About the Authors

Dr Basant K. Puri is Consultant Psychiatrist and Senior Lecturer at the MRI Unit for the Imperial College School of Medicine, and is Honorary Consultant in Imaging for Hammersmith Hospital's Department of Radiology. He is a leading expert in the use of EPA for depression and has been involved in medical research for about twelve years. His papers have been widely published in international journals and he has written several books.

Hilary Boyd was educated at Roedean and London University, and is a qualified nurse, trained at the world famous Hospital for Sick Children in Great Ormond Street, a marriage guidance counsellor, journalist and writer. A depression sufferer herself, she has a keen interest in the problems of depressive illness and has already written on the subject in her book *Banishing the Blues*. She has also written on mind, body, spirit issues in the *Express* newspaper, and is the author of *The Step-parent's Survival Guide* and *Working Woman's Pregnancy*.

D0281136

the NATURAL WAY
to beat DEPRESSION

Dr BASANT K. PURI
& HILARY BOYD

HODDER

MOBIUS

Hodder & Stoughton

This book is intended as a guide to people who want to improve and maintain their health. If you are concerned in any way about your health, you should seek medical advice.

Copyright © 2004 by Dr Basant K. Puri and Hilary Boyd

First published in Great Britain in 2004 by Hodder and Stoughton
A division of Hodder Headline

The right of Dr Basant K. Puri and Hilary Boyd to be identified as the Authors of the Work has been asserted by them in accordance with the Copyright, Designs and Patents Act 1988.

Diagram featured on p. 81 ©'Hibbeln J. R. 'LCPUFAs in depression and related conditions' in Peet M., Glen I. & Horrobin D. F. (eds.), *Phospholipid Spectrum Disorder in Psychiatry* (1st edition. Carnforth: Marius Press, 1999)

A Mobius Book

1 3 5 7 9 10 8 6 4 2

All rights reserved. No part of this publication may be reproduced, stored in a retrieval system, or transmitted, in any form or by any means without the prior written permission of the publisher, nor be otherwise circulated in any form of binding or cover other than that in which it is published and without a similar condition being imposed on the subsequent purchaser.

A CIP catalogue record for this title is available from the British Library

ISBN 0 340 82496 4

Typeset in Bembo by
Palimpsest Book Production Limited, Polmont, Stirlingshire

Printed and bound by
Clays Ltd, St Ives plc

Hodder and Stoughton
A division of Hodder Headline
338 Euston Road
London NW1 3BH

Contents

Foreword   vi

Introduction   vii

1. A Remarkable Breakthrough   I

2. What is Depression?   20

3. Why Do We Get Depressed?   54

4. How Can EPA Help?   87

5. Antidepressants versus Natural Treatments   112

6. Treating Depression with EPA   148

7. Everyone Can Benefit from EPA   185

8. Your Journey to Recovery   206

Glossary   232

Further Resources   237

Index   244

Foreword
by Professor Sir Graham Hills

This book by the distinguished medical scientist Dr Basant Puri will bring hope to the many people who suffer from the debilitating condition of depression. As one of the commonest aliments in adult life, depression afflicts a wide range of persons, irrespective of their social backgrounds, their incomes or their lifestyles – and for so long its origin was a mystery.

But now, advances in modern medicine have brought greater understanding to the complex nature of the brain. Medical scientists have now found ways to unravel the mystery of how the brain works and to investigate the very processes that cause depression. It may be triggered by events, it may be affected by diet, but whatever its cause, the brain can now be studied through such modern technologies as the scanner.

Dr Basant Puri is a leader in this field of brain science. He is that unusual medical scientist with a knowledge not just of clinical psychiatry but of the physics and chemistry of the brain as well as of the mathematical niceties of the new instrumentation. This extraordinarily powerful combination of insights is the basis of his medical procedures to diagnose, to study and to ameliorate depression.

I know Dr Basant Puri well. I have followed his researches closely, especially those into the diagnosis of depression. These researches are of the highest originality and they offer a new and sounder basis for the future diagnosis and treatment of this debilitating condition.

Introduction

Over the period of a month, in my early twenties, I noticed that a fellow medical student who lived next door to me was gradually changing for the worse. From being an affable, hard-working and highly intelligent young man who would normally have been out regularly punting along the River Cam, he had turned into a pale shadow of his former self. He had become an almost zombie-like creature, who had trouble with blurred vision, and had developed strange, rigid movements, and a fixed, forward-looking stare. When I would greet him in the morning, as we got ready to leave our student digs and make our way to the teaching hospital (Addenbrooke's), he could barely mumble good morning back. What had gone wrong?

It appeared my fellow student had been rejected in love and was suffering from depression, for which he was receiving treatment in the form of antidepressant medication. For the first time I was witnessing the debilitating side effects of anti-depressants, and it both surprised and shocked me. I could not help wondering why he had been prescribed such a powerful drug for what was more lovesickness than depression, and perhaps, unconsciously, this was the beginning of my interest in a more natural treatment for depressive illness.

A few years later my initial interest in antidepressants and their side effects was rekindled. I was back at Addenbrooke's Hospital as a fully qualified junior doctor now specialising in psychiatry and I was attending a lecture on antidepressants and other 'modern' psychiatric drugs from a senior and now world-famous psychiatrist named Dr David Healy. His theme was the many side effects of antidepressant medication, and he even actively questioned the underlying theories about how depression occurs and how it should be treated. This was not something I had read about in my textbooks, and at the time I wondered if the prevailing medical wisdom could be wrong. Surely there could not be a viable alternative to synthetic antidepressants, whatever their side effects.

However, it was to be years before I returned to my initial interest in the antidepressant story, which had been sparked by my student friend and then fanned by David Healy. After training in psychiatry and then training in neuroimaging, I came across the work of Professor David F. Horrobin and Professor Malcolm Peet on nutritional substances (essential fatty acids) to treat depression. From the evidence then available, and subsequent research, I and some of my colleagues began to see that one particular omega-3 fatty acid, EPA, stood head and shoulders above the others as a likely antidepressant. It was now just a matter of time before a clinician actually tried using EPA in this role.

I waited and waited. I telephoned Professor Horrobin and told him I was sure that EPA was having an antidepressant action in my patients with schizophrenia being treated with it. Still, no one seemed ready to try it therapeutically as an antidepressant. So in the end I took up the challenge myself. This book will detail the astonishing results that treating depression with EPA produced. Results that were followed up later with trials which confirmed that EPA works to lift even very serious depressive symptoms.

EPA has been found to be a highly successful, side-effect-free antidepressant, but in the course of our research, which has been continued by many fatty acid pioneers worldwide, we discovered that EPA is capable of improving brain function overall, and that the human body actually has a particular need for omega-3 essential fatty acids. It seems a deficiency is likely to lead to many of the clinical problems that are common in this day and age. I gradually became interested in this other dimension to EPA too, as it turned out from many research trials that EPA can be used successfully to help other serious conditions, such as heart disease, chronic fatigue syndrome and Huntington's disease, and is also of general benefit to our overall health and the health of our skin, hair and nails. This is as exciting a discovery as the depression research proved to be, and offers hope to those for whom conventional medicine has no answers.

Our Western diet and lifestyle have compromised our ability to make our own EPA. Factors such as caffeine (tea, coffee, chocolate), nicotine (smoking), stress hormones (from stressful daily living), high levels of trans-fatty acids (very common in modern processed foods), and certain vitamin and mineral deficiencies all conspire to make it difficult for our bodies to produce EPA and closely related omega-3 fatty acids. But now that we understand this, it is possible, as we detail in this book, to take a high-EPA nutritional supplement to replace the lost fatty acids so vital to our health and wellbeing.

I have worked extensively in the fields of essential fatty acid research and the benefit of EPA in treating brain disorders. As a result my name was destined to be strongly associated with EPA and depression. However I do not feel I deserved this. To paraphrase the well-known words of Sir Isaac Newton from a letter to Hooke, if I had appeared at that time to see a little further than some of my colleagues, it was merely because I had stood on the shoulders of giants. These pioneering giants were Professor David F. Horrobin, Professor Malcolm Peet, Dr Iain Glen and Professor Krishna Vaddadi. And, like so many pioneers, our path has not been an easy one, with the reaction from many of our colleagues in the psychiatric arena regarding our EPA research ranging from sceptical to downright scathing. But the fact is that EPA has been shown conclusively to work, and attitudes are slowly beginning to change as the evidence reaches a wider audience. One of the purposes of writing this book has been to bring our discovery of the huge potential of EPA not only to the attention of the medical profession, but also to the general public, so that everyone can benefit.

I should like to take this opportunity to thank Dr Iain Glen, Professor Malcolm Peet and Professor Krishna Vaddadi for many hours of stimulating discussions. Those who are used to reading academic papers and books authored by me may be pleasantly surprised at how readable the text of this book is. Alas, this is not another benefit of taking EPA! Rather, the credit must go to my co-author, Hilary Boyd, and Emma Heyworth-Dunn and Rowena Webb from Hodder and Stoughton, for taking on the task of converting my original version into what you see before you today; again, I extend them my warm thanks.

In March 2003 I had arranged to meet my close colleague and mentor Professor David Horrobin at an international conference in Colorado Springs. I duly travelled across the Atlantic to America in March, but alas David was too ill to attend. On 1 April 2003, while in the United States, I was devastated to learn that he had died. So, far from meeting up with him, instead, the following week I heard my name being called out to help carry his coffin at his funeral.

It is my earnest hope that the medical profession will become convinced of the importance of omega-3 essential fatty acid research, and that in due course natural safe therapies such as EPA will become widely available for debilitating conditions such as depression. This would certainly be a fitting legacy to the memory of Professor David Horrobin.

Basant K. Puri
Cambridge, 2003

Chapter One

A Remarkable Breakthrough

At last there is some good news for the many millions of people in the world today whose lives are blighted by depression. In the past two years, consultant and senior lecturer Dr Basant Puri and an international group of medical scientists investigating mental disorders have come up with a remarkable body of research which heralds a breakthrough in the treatment of depression. This research turns many of the commonly held beliefs about the causes and treatment of this illness on their heads.

Dr Puri has discovered mounting evidence with patients in his clinical practice that a particular substance found in fish oils, called eicosapentaenoic acid (EPA), can significantly alleviate the symptoms of depression, even in its most severe form. His research is backed up by the use of advanced brain-scanning techniques which highlight the extraordinary benefits this substance has on regenerating the brain. Treatment options to date for a person suffering from this debilitating disease have involved antidepressant drugs which carry a heavy burden of possible side effects, but EPA is a naturally occurring substance and has no adverse side effects; in fact exactly the opposite.

This book sets out to explain the complexities of depressive illness, and to tell the story of how this revolutionary new research came about and the struggles the research scientists encountered in progressing their research. Most importantly, it explains what this breakthrough means to the millions currently afflicted with depression worldwide, and how you can incorporate natural EPA into your life to give you health and wellbeing both now and in the years to come.

Depression is an Illness

Depression is a truly disabling disease, and for those who suffer from it, it is a clearly defined condition. Even if the experience of depression sufferers varies in the detail, such as the degree or longevity of their illness, or the precise symptoms they experience, the core feeling of ongoing despair and hopelessness is always the same.

Depression is not just feeling low; depression is to a low mood what flu is to the common cold. Every winter people catch a cold virus, feel rough for a week, and go around telling all their friends that they've had flu. But if you have ever experienced real flu, you will know that there is an enormous difference. The same is true of depression. We all have weeks when things are going wrong in our life. It might be the split-up of a relationship, a work or financial worry, a sick relative. But our low mood is attached to the moment, and the moment passes, usually quite quickly, perhaps helped by a night out with some friends, or a chat with a family member. These feelings are valid, and they can be painful and hard to cope with at the time, but they are not the same as depression. The trouble with depression is that, if you have never experienced it, it is a very difficult disease to understand. This is true of the relatives and friends of a depressed person, and it is also often true of the medical practitioners faced with a depressed patient. Partly this is because no one has yet definitively pinpointed the cause of depression, and also because the symptoms and severity, not to mention the progress and outcome of the illness, vary so much from person to person.

You could say the same of cancer, yet cancer, rightly or wrongly, is categorised as a mechanical disease, a disease where the normal, regulatory mechanism for cell growth has become damaged. Depression, on the other hand, is seen as a mental disorder with an emotional component. Not only is our Western society fearful of any form of mental distress, or so-called 'madness', but also a depressed person is to some degree still held responsible for his or her condition in a way that a cancer sufferer is not – unless they have a forty-a-day smoking habit.

Depression is deemed embarrassing, both for the sufferer and for their relatives. There is a perceived wisdom that those who suffer from the illness are displaying an inherent weakness, a personality flaw. This stigma of mental illness persists, and makes it more difficult for a depressed person to ask for, and receive, the appropriate treatment. It has been found that around two-thirds of people in the UK suffering from major depression are never correctly diagnosed, and therefore never treated for depression.

The Broader Picture

Yet everyone is talking about depression these days. We are told it is now reaching epidemic proportions in the Western world, particularly in the United States, with the World Health Organisation (WHO) warning us that by 2020 major depression is set to come second on the list of diseases that present the most acute international health burden, causing disability and early death, lost man hours and taking up valuable medical resources. It is even overtaking cancer, malaria and AIDS, with only chronic heart disease a bigger problem in the Western world. Studies show that between 15 and 30 per cent of the world's population will suffer a depressive episode at some time in their life. And depression has also been linked to the other diseases that rank high on the list, such as heart disease and cancer.

This level of disability worldwide has a high cost. Not just in hard cash, but in the wider social implication of families wrenched apart by the disease and what this means in the long term for those families both emotionally and financially. If these alarming statistics are a true picture of depression in today's world, what does it mean? Are we all sliding inexorably into a pit of depressive illness, and if so, why and what can we do about it?

Many modern social factors have been blamed for the increase in depression. For instance, job insecurity, isolation from the family support network because of economic migration, lack of religious belief, the high divorce rate, general life stress from modern technology, pollution and the speed at which we choose to live, and greater access to drugs and alcohol, particularly in the young and vulnerable. It seems that life has got more complicated, and some of us are less equipped to deal with it than others.

The Research

Unfortunately, these factors are not easy to change overnight, but alongside social factors, depression is also thought to have a significant biological component, and it is on this that the main thrust of medical research targeting depression has been concentrating in recent years, specifically on the action of brain chemicals, or neurotransmitters, such as serotonin and noradrenaline, and their effect on our moods. Low levels of neurotransmitters are strongly associated with depression, although they have not been proved to be the cause of it, and play only one role among many in the depression story.

Because antidepressant drugs, given the size of this burgeoning health problem, presented a potentially big money-spinner for the drug companies, millions of dollars were, and still are, ploughed into the creation of drugs that increase the levels of these neurotransmitters in the brain. The older antidepressants that addressed this problem, each in different ways, such as tricyclics and monoamine oxidase inhibitors (MAOIs), were the drugs of choice for doctors treating depression until the 1990s. These drugs were, and indeed still are, often successful in treating depressive illness, particularly the severe form of the disease, but they have unpleasant, even if short-term, side effects which many people find hard to tolerate. Then in the late 1980s a new anti-depressant drug class took the market by storm.

This class, called Selective Serotonin Re-uptake Inhibitors (SSRIs), the first trade-named being Prozac, was a big success story, making billions for the drug companies. It was initially thought to have few side effects, and it quickly became known as the 'happy pill'. But then worrying reports began to emerge, albeit not extensive at first, suggesting a potential link between the use of SSRIs and suicidal and violent tendencies – although no causal relationships has been estab-lished. What is certain, however, is that there is a long list of less life-threatening, but none the less problematic, symptoms associated with SSRIs, including nausea, insomnia, weight loss or gain, and loss of libido and ability to achieve orgasm.

The honeymoon was over, leaving people with depression, and their doctors, the unenviable task of deciding whether to risk the potential side effects or not in their attempt to alleviate depression. Even the market leader in alternative treatments for the illness, St John's Wort, has now generated research which suggests that if given in high doses it can react badly with sunlight, possibly causing eye damage. It is also thought to have the potential for raising blood pressure, and reducing the effect of some low-dose oral contraceptives, although the herb has not yet been subjected to extensive enough research to validate these contentions.

The Way Forward

Luckily, however, out of this morass of conflicting inform-ation and worrying treatment options for depression stepped a group of medical scientists, one of whom was Dr Basant Puri, with what was to prove a revolutionary idea. Based on research done over thirty years ago by a medical researcher called Professor David Horrobin, these doctors decided to conduct a study in which a group of patients suffering from schizophrenia were randomly allocated the fish oil derivative EPA, or a placebo. The unexpected side effect experienced by the schizophrenic patients taking the fish oils was that their symptoms of depression – which often accompany schizo-phrenia – cleared within weeks. Dr Puri then decided to put this theory to practical application with his own patients. Here is an account of Dr Puri's first case study in which EPA was used as a treatment specifically for depression.

ANTHONY'S STORY

One afternoon in 1996 a mother and her son arrived in my consulting room for an appointment. The mother looked deeply anxious, the adult son sat slumped in his chair, silent and looking at the floor. The young man, Anthony, had apparently been suffering from severe clinical depression since the age of fourteen. Over the past seven years his doctors had prescribed virtually every known antidepressant drug treatment, including combinations of drugs, but nothing had been in any way effective. He had been referred to me in the hope that I might have some other treatment suggestions that had not already been tried.

I could see clearly that Anthony was in a bad way. Now twenty-one, he was a tall, dark-haired young man whose clothes hung loosely on his lean frame, suggesting that he had lost weight. Like many people suffering from depression, he found it difficult to make eye contact and spoke hesitantly and quietly.

I began by giving Anthony a physical examination to exclude other possible causes for his depressed state, as there are some diseases that cause depressive symptoms. Was he depressed because of anaemia? No, his fingernails were not a pallid, anaemic colour. Was he suffering from a thyroid disorder? No, this was unlikely since he did not have the characteristic facial features of either too much or too little circulating thyroid hormones, there was no obvious goitrous mass in his neck and his hands were not manifesting a tremor and were a normal temperature. Perhaps he was suffering from Addison's disease, a rare hormone problem that my colleagues in the medical profession sometimes misdiagnose as depression? If he did have Addison's then more than likely the creases of his palms would be dark, but there was no sign of this. And finally I checked his arms for evidence of injection marks from using illegal drugs, but there were none. After taking a full medical history and carrying out a thorough physical examination of Anthony, I was able to confirm that he was indeed suffering from depression.

Anthony and his mother told me that his condition had grown steadily worse over the years, despite different treatments, and that the last two years had been particularly tough for him. Somehow he had continued to go to school and even attended college, but he had found it hard to study and to take part in any of the college activities such as sport or a social life. He often spent hours and even days just lying on his bed feeling miserable and low, unable to carry on any semblance of a normal life. And because he found it difficult to make friends or even to spend time with others, preferring to be alone with his low mood, he became increasingly isolated.

Anthony also had several other classic symptoms of depression. His sleep patterns were disrupted. He might go to sleep, but then wake very early in the morning and not be able to get to sleep again. He had lost his appetite and as a result had lost weight, he found it difficult to concentrate on his work, and as a result was in danger of dropping out of college, and, most crucially, he frequently felt suicidal. Obviously his parents were deeply worried about their son and had taken him to their GP and then to a number of specialists, who had prescribed several different types of antidepressants, none of which had really helped. It was clear that Anthony had what is known as resistant depression, the severest form of the illness and one that does not respond to treatment.

Anthony's suicidal thoughts were of particular concern to me. They were very intense and he spent some time explaining why he felt that life was not worth living any more. He was seriously considering killing himself, and had narrowed down the possible methods to two preferred options. As I listened to this articulate, intelligent young man put forward his arguments, I felt deeply saddened. The issue uppermost in my mind was Anthony's safety. I seriously considered whether it might be necessary to hospitalise him. However, after careful discussion with Anthony's mother, she was able to assure me that she would keep a close eye on him, and remove all potentially dangerous items that could be used in an attempt to commit suicide. She also promised to contact the appropriate services and me immediately if she thought Anthony was in imminent danger of killing himself. On this basis, I decided that he should not be admitted to hospital.

So how was I to treat him? How could I help in a case where all the major textbook treatments for depression had been tried unsuccessfully? In the back of my mind I had an idea, a treatment I believed just might work for Anthony. But it hadn't been tried before on depression, so Anthony would have to agree to be a test case. Could I ask him and his mother to agree to such a thing, given the degree of his depression and suicidal thoughts? I explained to them what I had in mind.

The treatment was eicosapentaenoic acid, or EPA, which is a derivative of a naturally occurring essential fatty acid (EFA). The richest source of this omega-3 fatty acid is oily fish, including salmon, tuna (not tinned), mackerel, pilchards and sardines. But what I had in mind was a highly purified form of EPA, which could deliver a higher dose than you would get from just eating oily fish. My belief that EPA might help Anthony was based in part on a large trial of patients with schizophrenia which had recently taken place. I was one of the doctors running the trial and several of my patients had taken part. Three-quarters of the patients had been given EPA in varying doses, while the others were given a placebo, which is a pill containing no medication. It was a double-blind trial, meaning that neither the doctor administering the treatment, nor the patient receiving it, knew who was being given EPA and who the placebo.

Patients suffering from schizophrenia are often depressed and one of the most striking things I had noticed in the study was that the symptoms of depression cleared in many of the patients taking EPA. This had led me to think about using EPA as a treatment for depression. But could it help Anthony? Could it improve his intractable depression when nothing else had? I believed it could. But I had to admit to Anthony and his mother that there were no published studies of EPA as a treatment specifically for depression to date. So Anthony would be the first.

Anthony's mother was naturally a little unsure about trying a treatment on her son which had not been tried on anyone before. I was able to reassure her that EPA is a naturally occurring food substance and would be entirely safe for her son to take, with no adverse side effects. I would give it to him alongside his prescribed antidepressant medication, because although his current treatments were not alleviating his symptoms, it could be dangerous to stop taking the drugs suddenly.

On this basis, Anthony and his mother agreed to go ahead with EPA. I gave him a highly purified form of a particular derivative of EPA, known as ethyl-EPA, and then carefully monitored the results. Anthony also agreed to allow me to run several highly specialised tests, including brain scans, in order to observe the effects of the EPA.

The Breakthrough

Nine months later, Anthony and his mother were once again in my consulting room. This time they were both smiling and his mother was thanking me effusively and declaring that a miracle had taken place.

I could see for myself that Anthony was transformed. He appeared a confident, self-assured young man who shook my hand warmly and who had no problem looking me in the eye. All the signs of depression had gone. He was eating and sleeping well, and enjoying catching up with his studies and his social life. His suicidal thoughts had completely disappeared and he was excited about his plans for the future, which included a period of study in America and setting up his own company. Anthony and his mother told me that within two to three months of starting the ethyl-EPA all his depressive symptoms had cleared. After seven years of struggle against the tyranny of this unremitting disease, Anthony had at last won back his health and his will to live. I was absolutely delighted. It was wonderful to see Anthony so well and to find that EPA had been such a success.

A few days after this visit, I finished analysing Anthony's brain scans. I compared the brain scan I had taken after the course of EPA with the one taken nine months earlier before treatment began. The results were astonishing.

Because Anthony was already an adult, I would not expect to see any change in the brain structure over a nine-month period. If he had started to develop a brain disease such as dementia, in which he was losing nerve cells and cerebral tissue, then I would expect to see that the two largest brain ventricles, or chambers, had become larger as the brain deteriorated. In fact what I saw was the opposite process. Anthony's brain ventricles had become smaller and parts of his cerebral cortex had become thicker – both changes that pointed to the possibility that regrowth might have taken place in parts of his brain. It used to be taught as fact in medical schools that the human brain, in an adult, is not capable of further growth. Since then it has been proven that the adult mammalian brain does have the capacity to regenerate its cells, though we still know little about this process. The results of Anthony's brain scans led me to believe in the possibility that EPA can, in some way, stimulate stem cells in our brains to produce new nerve cells, offering hope for a variety of conditions that adversely affect the brain.

Hope for All Depression Sufferers

Dr Puri's breakthrough in successfully treating such a severe case of depression as Anthony's with EPA made him realise that the same treatment might also be applied to the less serious, but none the less debilitating, cases of depression that doctors and patients are faced with on a daily basis. At the time of writing this book, he has used EPA to alleviate symptoms successfully in an ever-growing number of the depression sufferers he sees in his clinical practice.

Scepticism towards the Theory

Dr Puri and his colleagues have faced considerable doubt concerning their research, something that is common with many new theories. Dr Barry Marshall, for instance, the doctor who was responsible for research identifying the helibacter-pylori organism implicated in many stomach ulcers, took ten years to persuade a sceptical medical and pharmaceutical establishment that ulcers caused by this organism could be treated with a combination of antibiotics. Part of Dr Marshall's problem, as with Dr Puri, was that most medical research is funded by drug companies, and the companies had invested a great deal of money in the acid-inhibitors currently being used as the main weapon in healing stomach ulcers.

For nearly thirty years Professor Horrobin's research into schizophrenia had been marginalised, and the new EPA champions have also been laughed out of court by their peers. They have also been met with a distinct lack of enthusiasm by pharmaceutical companies – not least because EPA is not a new, patentable drug but an already existing natural substance. So no money has been forthcoming from any drug company to support their research efforts. But the scientists were not deterred, and recently, in the light of their joint research studies and documented evidence in some of the major international psychiatric journals, the atmosphere has been changing, to the point where their research is now entering mainstream medical thinking.

How *The Natural Way to Beat Depression* Can Help You

When you are suffering from depression you can feel very bewildered and confused. What is depression? How has this happened to me? How can I get better? These are the key questions to which you want answers. So you will be looking to this book to explain the whys and wherefores of your illness and how taking EPA will restore you to health both now and in the long term. Here are the topics we cover, which we hope will give you all the information you need to understand and cope with your depression.

DEBUNKING THE MYTHS

The first aim of this book is to demystify depression. Because so many of us are both frightened and ignorant of what mental illness entails, depression has long been shrouded in myths and fancies. For instance, the abiding myth that someone who is depressed can 'snap out of it' if they really tried. Or the idea that depression necessarily bears any relation to the current circumstances of a person's life. 'How can she be depressed when she has a lovely house, plenty of money and a loving husband and children?' Or the conviction among many that if you have suffered from depression at any time this makes you mentally weak and unreliable. This book debunks these unhelpful attitudes.

1. Understanding depressive illness

This book aims to explain the circumstances of depression in the light of current research, explaining symptoms and their possible causes and bringing together the various components, such as the biological, social and physical factors, that are present when someone is suffering from depressive illness. We look at mild, moderate and severe depression, including bipolar disorder, postnatal depression and seasonal affective disorder (SAD).

In order to obtain successful treatment for a condition, it is important to understand as much as you can about what is happening in your body and your mind. If you don't understand the pathology of a disease and its treatment you can be prey to other people's ignorance and dangerous advice, and also to your own possibly frightening fancies. For instance, how do you know when you are depressed? How do you know when to seek help? What should you expect when you go to the doctor with a list of your symptoms? How long might your depressive illness last?

The Internet is a popular source of information about

health issues these days, but beware the casual soundbite without any qualified medical background, which leaves you more confused than when you started. This book deals comprehensively with all aspects of depression from a professionally qualified standpoint.

2. Who is affected and why?

This book investigates who gets depressed and why some of us are more susceptible to the illness than others. We look at the genetic component, the psychological factor – which includes the childhood blueprints that give us a poor sense of our own worth and are thought to be a contributory factor in depression – and the gender issue: women are thought to be at least two to three times more likely to suffer from depression than men.

3. Current treatment options

If you are currently being treated for depression, you will want to know what the implications are for your treatment in the light of Dr Puri's new research. Obviously it is dangerous to stop taking a course of antidepressant drugs suddenly without medical supervision, but the good news is that EPA can be taken alongside your current medication as a supplementary treatment. The book includes up-to-date information about antidepressant medication and the potential side effects, profiles of the natural alternatives other than EPA, such as St John's Wort, and suggestions for diet regimes to help your body to optimum health. We also describe the purpose of the various tests, such as brain scans, that may be carried out.

4. The theory behind the new treatment

We detail Professor David Horrobin's theory which has brought Dr Puri and others to discover the essential fatty acid derivative, EPA, as a treatment to relieve depressive symptoms. It will take us back millions of years to the origins of the human brain.

5. What is EPA and where do we find it?

The body's chemistry, with its amazing interaction of proteins, fats, fatty acids, amino acids, hormones and brain chemicals, is an extremely complex system, so to understand why EFAs feed the brain, we do need a little science! However, the aim of this book is to explain rather than burden you with complicated physiology, so we have kept the scientific explanations simplified and accessible.

This book explains exactly what essential fatty acids are, why it is difficult for the body to make its own EFAs, and how the body uses them from the food we eat. It also explains EPA, and why this particular EFA is thought to be the best treatment for depressive symptoms. We outline the natural food sources of EFAs, the poor dietary habits which might compromise the body's absorption of them, and general dietary hints to achieve optimum mental health. EPA has many other health benefits, and we tell you about these too.

6. Getting treatment with EPA

The book outlines the best course to follow if you want either to supplement your diet with EPA, or you require professional help with depression and would like to know how to persuade your practitioner to prescribe it. If you are currently being treated for depression you will almost certainly be taking antidepressant drugs, which you will be depending on to make you better. You will have been persuaded both by your doctor and by information you have received through friends and the media that this is the only way to alleviate your miserable symptoms. These drugs, in your vulnerable state, will feel like your lifeline, so you might be understandably suspicious of someone telling you they have a natural treatment which you can use instead of your heavyweight drugs. This is a perfectly reasonable position, especially in the light of so much New Age promise of 'natural' cures for all our ills.

But Dr Puri's EPA discovery is based on solid scientific research, trials and clinical experience carried out by him and other highly qualified doctors and scientists. The beauty of this natural substance is that, although Dr Puri prescribes it instead of antidepressants to relieve his patients' symptoms, you can also take it alongside your current treatment, just as Anthony did, or as your drugs are being gradually reduced, and still reap the benefit of this breakthrough discovery. We explain the ins and outs of how you can use EPA, how much you need, and whether you need to take it as a general supplement to ward off possible depressive episodes in the future. And because EPA is contained in the food we eat, we take you through some easy steps to increase levels of EPA in your body through your daily diet.

WHO WILL BENEFIT FROM *THE NATURAL WAY TO BEAT DEPRESSION*?

This book is written for many different groups of people.
1. For people who think they might be depressed. Read on and you will get a clear picture of what your symptoms might imply, who you should go to for help and when, what that help might be, and when you can expect to see some improvement in your condition with EPA.

2. For those who are depressed but are frightened to go to their doctor because they don't want to be put on anti-depressant drugs. If you know you can take EPA, perhaps the decision to seek help will be easier.

3. For people already suffering from depression, who want to expand their knowledge of the disease and take full advantage of the new research within, or instead of, their existing treatment regime. (Don't forget, it is important not to stop your course of antidepressants without medical advice.) And for those who are badly affected by the side effects of anti-depressant medication and want a natural alternative.

4. For anyone who is related to, working with, or a friend of a person they think might be experiencing a depressive illness, or close to someone who is already in treatment for one. There is nothing more worrying and upsetting than watching someone you love distintegrating and not knowing how to help. This book will give you all the information you need to support such a person.

5. For GPs at the front line of depression treatment. This book will provide all the information about Dr Puri's revolutionary new treatment, so that doctors can offer the most successful range of options for their depressed patients.

6. For anyone interested in a new theory and a new treatment for a disease that is making such a significant mark on today's Western world.

We hope that reading this book will be a comforting experience as well as an informative one. Depression is such an isolating condition, and many of us are afraid of seeking help because we fear the treatment almost as much as the disease, fuelled by the endless scare stories which involve almost all the current crop of antidepressant drugs. Now there is a viable, natural alternative to those heavyweight drugs, with a high rate of success, perhaps you will find it easier to seek treatment. The frightening American statistic that 70 per cent of people never have their depression diagnosed or treated says it all. But depression is a disease like any other, and deserves the best treatment currently available. We hope that this book will encourage you to get the help that you deserve.

Chapter Two

What is Depression?

The importance of the medical breakthrough outlined in this book is borne out by some of the statistics we have listed below which currently relate to depressive illness. Statistics are notoriously difficult to read and should always be taken with a pinch of salt, but they are none the less an interesting indicator of the trend in depressive illness as a worldwide problem. The findings may seem alarming, first because we are not used to seeing depression as a killer disease in the way we have been taught to regard cancer and heart disease in the Western industrialised world, and second because the diagnosis and treatment of depression still seem to be rather a hit-and-miss affair, with so many people undiagnosed, and others not responding to the treatment on offer, either because the drugs don't work, or they don't take them properly, or they cannot tolerate the unpleasant side effects of antidepressant medication.

- Approximately one in five people in Britain suffers from depression at some time in their life, but nearly two-thirds do not get help or treatment either because it is not recognised, or they are so disabled they cannot access help, or they are blamed for personal weakness, or they are misdiagnosed and wrongly treated for a medical problem.

- As many as 2.9 million people in Britain are diagnosed as having depression at any one time.
- Some 20 per cent of patients visiting their GPs have depressive symptoms, but nearly half of these may go unrecognised.
- In a recent survey, 23 per cent of the British public thought that a depressed person was dangerous to others.
- With diagnosis and appropriate treatment, over 80 per cent of depressed people can feel better within weeks.
- At least 30 per cent of people on antidepressants don't take their drugs properly, or prematurely discontinue their medication, often suddenly rather than gradually.
- More than half of the people who have had one episode of major depression will have another at some point.
- Suicide is the third leading cause of death among young people aged 15–24. Young men have the fastest rising suicide rate, up 85 per cent between 1980 and 1990. More than two young people commit suicide every day in Britain and Ireland.
- Depressed men are more than twice as likely to develop coronary heart disease as their non-depressed counterparts.

Faced with these statistics, it seems vital that we finally get to grips with depression by being as informed as possible about the symptoms and progress of this difficult disease. The more understanding we have, the better the chances of removing the taboo that hangs over the condition, and the more likely that a climate will grow where depression sufferers no longer feel ashamed about their symptoms, allowing them to access the help they need. Especially now, when there is a real chance that their symptoms can be alleviated with a natural, side-effect-free alternative to antidepressant medication.

Defining Depression

Depression is a term used to describe a wide range of mood disorders that create psychological distress in the sufferer. The illness can ebb and flow, the severity of symptoms can be erratic, being sometimes mild, sometimes very bad, sometimes almost bearable for a while – during which time the symptoms appear to recede – then often returning even worse than before. It can last for just a few weeks, or for months and even years.

There are broadly two categories of depression: the reactive type, which comes on as a result of some external circumstance, such as the death of someone close to you, losing a job, divorce or chronic illness; and clinical depression, which is depression that is mainly biological in origin. The origins of clinical depression are still not clear, but Dr Puri's research throws new light on the factors previously thought to trigger depressive illness. Within these two broad categories there are more specific classifications for depression which are used by doctors to facilitate diagnosis and treatment: mild, moderate and severe. The classifications are based on the number and degree of symptoms – of which there are many – present in a patient at any one time. These are only guidelines, and many patients spill over from one category to another or progress from, say, moderate to severe depression. Few fit neatly into one classification and no two depressions are identical.

As well as the type of depression and the degree to which the patient is suffering, there is often a context in which the person is depressed, such as those affected by seasonal light deprivation (SAD), postnatal depression and bipolar disorder, or manic depression.

What Does It Feel Like to Be Depressed?

As we said earlier, depressive illness is very different from the sort of low mood that you might experience when something difficult or unpleasant is happening in your life, or you are merely going through a boring, uneventful period where there seems to be nothing exciting to look forward to. These low moods are part of everyday life; it is not the human condition to be in a state of perpetual happiness, despite what some magazines would have you believe. But for most of us these low moods are fleeting, and can be easily dispelled by such strategies as talking the problem through with a friend or family member, finding a new job, a new relationship, or taking a break from routine. And a low mood still allows you to get enjoyment from simple things, like seeing your child laugh, or trying on a new pair of shoes. In fact you can 'snap out of' a low mood, you can even 'pull yourself together' if need be.

Depression is different. You might not even realise that you are depressed, because the feeling is so utterly alien to a normal mood, and can sneak up on you insidiously and without warning, changing your ability to see things clearly. You might feel bewildered, mad even, and blame your deep reluctance to get out of bed, or to do anything, or to speak to anyone, on the fact that you are undisciplined, weak and useless. You might convince yourself that you have a terminal disease which might explain your extreme symptoms. You might just think that the world as you know it has come to an end, and that no one else has noticed. You will almost undoubtedly feel hopeless, exhausted and ashamed. These feelings, as you can see, are not the feelings we so often get from a passing low mood.

The Symptoms of Depression

The symptoms of depression vary widely from person to person in their number, severity and duration, making it hard for the sufferer, the people close to the sufferer and the practitioner faced with the sufferer to make a firm diagnosis. This is further complicated by the fact that certain diseases can mimic depressive symptoms, thus throwing the doctor off the scent. Depression symptoms might present suddenly, or they might creep up on you gradually, and during the course of a depressive episode the symptoms might vary. Here is a list of the possible symptoms a person suffering from depression might experience.

1. Persistent low mood

This is the number one depression symptom. We have discussed the difference between a low mood and a low depressive mood, but the best way to describe this depressed feeling is by imagining a mood scale of one to ten. Happiness is ten. A low mood is five. A serious trauma such as bereavement is two. A low depressive mood is zero. In its severest form it is off the scale of feeling because what the sufferer feels is nothing, just a persistent deadness, as if the world were going on in a separate place. And unlike a normal low mood, the feeling doesn't go away.

2. Feelings of despair and hopelessness

These feelings are a corollary to the persistent low mood and can often be frightening. It seems as if there is no hope of anything ever being any better. The future is bleak, the present unbearable, there seems to be no point to your life, yet at the same time you know that the reality of your life does not merit this despair. You may in fact have what others, and indeed you yourself, would consider a good life, but when you are depressed you just can't see it as good. And, worse, you cannot explain why you feel this way, so guilt is added to the mix of feelings. You can burst into tears at the smallest thing, or even for no apparent reason at all.

3. Loss of interest and pleasure in life
Things that previously gave you pleasure, and which you know should give you pleasure, no longer do. You usually love taking your children to the park, or going to a movie, or even just making your first cup of coffee of the day. But now you feel no sense of enjoyment or anticipation for any of these events.

4. Lack of energy
The torpor that falls over you like a blanket when you are depressed is extraordinary. You just cannot be bothered to do anything. Under the duvet seems the safest place, and even the smallest task, such as writing a letter or washing your hair, seems almost insuperable. Your sleep patterns are probably disturbed, but this does not entirely explain this overwhelming tiredness.

5. Disturbed sleep patterns
These vary; some depressed people, particularly those experiencing seasonal light deprivation depression or those with chronic depressive illness, tend to sleep too much. But the most common complaint with an acutely depressed person

is that, although they have no problem falling asleep, they tend to wake very early in the morning – 4 or 5 a.m. – and then can't get back to sleep. This is particularly distressing, not only because you feel alone and isolated when no one else is awake, but also you face the day already tired, with the knowledge that by the end of the day you will be exhausted. And this form of sleep disturbance is not cured by staying awake longer at night to make yourself extra tired.

6. Difficulty concentrating and making decisions

When you are depressed you find it hard to think clearly. Part of the problem is that you cannot concentrate on what is being said or what you are reading. You might read a paragraph over and over again and still have no idea what it means, or you might be talking to someone and suddenly be aware that you haven't heard a word of what they have just said. This is obviously very hard to cope with in a work situation, where you may appear flustered and incompetent to your colleagues, take longer to complete work assignments and find making decisions just too difficult.

7. Feeling worthless

This crisis in personal confidence leads on from the tiredness, lack of concentration and hopelessness. You begin to blame yourself. This is all my fault, you tell yourself. If I was cleverer, prettier, thinner, more successful I wouldn't be feeling this way. You begin to think that everyone is looking down on you, from your family to your work colleagues and even the waiter in the coffee shop. They can see you are a worthless person and nothing anyone can say will change your mind. In fact you might even think that your friends' attempts to console you are hollow and insincere. These feelings of worthlessness can increase your isolation, because day-to-day events such as getting together with friends, attending important work-related meetings, or even picking up your child from school become almost impossible to face.

8. Anxiety and panic attacks

You can be anxious without being depressed, but depressed people often manifest a high degree of anxiety. You might even experience panic attacks, when your heart starts racing, you break out in a sweat and find it difficult to breathe. You may become frightened to go out for no reason, or become over-sensitive to your environment; for instance a crowded room can unexpectedly make you nervous. Or you may experience sudden phobias, such as agoraphobia (a fear of going out in public places or travelling by public transport) or of heights – a steep escalator in a station can present a real problem for you. Or you may adopt what is known as obsessive/compulsive behaviour, where you wash yourself and your surroundings continuously, or you find you need to follow a specific ritual to complete tasks. These anxiety symptoms are not always experienced in depressive illness, but they are very common.

9. Appetite changes

Your eating habits sometimes change when you are depressed. You may eat too much and put on weight, treating food as the only reliable comfort in your life. Then as soon as you've eaten the food you become disgusted with yourself, and your added weight further reduces your self-esteem. Alternatively you may go off food and lose a lot of weight. You are still hungry, but as soon as the food is in front of you your appetite disappears and the thought of eating it makes you feel nauseous.

10. Impatience and irritability
You might feel like screaming at everyone and it's hard to stop yourself from doing so. And the more others try and reason with you and encourage you, the more they drive you mad.

11. Loss of libido
Like everything else, sex suddenly seems completely uninteresting. Whatever your sex drive previously, now you feel no desire for anyone. This can be problematic in a relationship, as the other person may not understand that your lack of desire has nothing whatever to do with them.

12. Persistent negative thoughts
This is a general feeling of negativity towards the whole world. You may begin to feel that your friends are selfish, that your partner doesn't love you any more, that your work colleague is being favoured by the boss, that your clothes are all gross. Everything and everyone is against you, but this negativity is not based in any reality.

13. Self-destructive behaviour
It is easy when faced with these bewildering mood alterations to seek some way of distancing yourself from your distress, and many people suffering from depression turn to excessive and uncharacteristic use of alcohol or drugs in the mistaken belief that they will find respite, or simply to get through the day. In the short term your despair may be forgotten, but when you return to reality the depression is still there and might feel even worse when mixed with the toxic residue of a hangover. You may also increase your nicotine intake, or take up smoking again.

14. Psychotic symptoms

This is a term used to describe a feature of severe depression when a person suffers from strange, illogical, false beliefs. You might hear voices that are not heard by others, or hallucinate – i.e. see things that are not there – or smell odours that no one else can smell. For instance, you might believe that a voice is telling you to burn all your possessions, or you might believe that your partner is trying to murder you.

15. Suicidal thoughts

You may think of suicide a lot, even planning the best way to kill yourself. Part of you wants to die because there is no point in living; another part is sure that you will be doing everyone a favour by removing your useless presence from the world. And yet, unless you are suffering from a severe form of depression, another part of you knows this isn't true and that your family and friends would be devastated if you were to kill yourself.

How is Depression Diagnosed?

Faced with this bewildering array of symptoms, how is a doctor to decide that their patient is definitively depressed and not just going through a stressful period in their life which is affecting, say, their sleep patterns? It is easy for a time-pressed GP to treat individual symptoms instead of spotting the wider problem. For instance, a patient may present with sleeping difficulties and be prescribed sleeping pills, which will do nothing to alleviate their depression.

There are, however, various physical changes in a person's appearance that may point to depression, and which a doctor can be alert to at the first examination. These include:

- Facial changes such as downturned eyes, sagging at the corners of the mouth and a furrow between the brows.
- The patient may avoid looking the doctor in the eye.
- Changes in overall appearance, for instance weight loss, poor self-care and general neglect such as grubby clothes and poor personal hygiene.
- Changes in speech patterns. Speech is typically slow, with long delays before questions are answered and poor concentration on any task.

Diagnostic Classification

Apart from listening to the symptoms described and observing the patient, there have also been specific diagnostic criteria created by experts to help doctors define depression. The two most important are those produced by the American Psychiatric Association (APA) and the World Health Organisation (WHO).

The APA classification is known as the *Diagnostic and Statistical Manual of Mental Disorders* (DSM), current edition DSM-IV-TR. It states that a person suffering a major depressive episode will present with at least five of the symptoms numbered 1–15 in the previous section during the same two-week period, and that these must be different from the person's usual mood. At least one of the symptoms must be an ongoing depressed mood or loss of pleasure in life. The sufferer will be showing an inability to function normally in a social, relationship or work environment, and their mood will not be as a result of inappropriate use of drugs, alcohol, medication or a medical condition.

The WHO classification is known as the *International Classification of Diseases and Related Health Problems*, abbreviated to ICD, the latest edition known as ICD-10. This is the one used by many National Health Service hospitals in the UK. It is more complicated than the APA system, but broadly speaking it divides depression into the three categories of mild, moderate and severe, and then further divides the symptoms into an A and B list. List A includes: ongoing depressed mood, loss of interest and enjoyment in life, tiredness and lethargy (numbers 1–3 listed above on pages 24–25). List B includes: all the other symptoms of depression listed above (numbers 4–15). There is also a C list, which is concerned with whether the general symptoms of depression are accompanied by psychotic symptoms such as hallucinations and delusions.

MILD DEPRESSION DIAGNOSED

A person with mild depression has at least two symptoms from List A and two from List B. None of List B should be too severe and the symptoms should have been ongoing for at least two weeks. The person affected will still be working and functioning at home, but with reduced usefulness and they will be experiencing no enjoyment in their daily tasks.

MODERATE DEPRESSION DIAGNOSED

A person with moderate depression has at least two symptoms from List A and at least three, preferably four, from List B, with several of the symptoms present to a marked degree, or a large number of symptoms present. The symptoms will have been experienced for at least two weeks. The person affected will be finding work very difficult, or may even have given it up, and will have become isolated from their family and normal social network.

SEVERE DEPRESSION DIAGNOSED

A person with severe depression has all the symptoms from List A and at least four from List B, which will be severe in intensity, lasting at least two weeks. The person affected will be unable to function normally any more. They will be suffering from marked low self-esteem and feelings of hopelessness and guilt. They might be experiencing psychotic symptoms such as hallucinations and delusions and be at a serious risk of committing suicide.

Problems with Diagnosis

The diagnostic criteria above, although sound when applied professionally, can only be put into practice if the person presenting with depression is able to articulate his symptoms. Many cannot. Another problem is that a depressed person, as the statistics show, will more than likely not seek professional help at all. In addition, the symptoms of depression can seem similar to the symptoms of certain medical conditions, such as anaemia, thyroid disorders and cancer, or may be masked by already existing medical problems, such as irritable bowel syndrome (IBS), chronic fatigue syndrome (CFS) and chronic migraine.

Patients don't want to be diagnosed with depression. They would rather be told they were suffering from what they consider a more 'presentable' disease, such as anaemia, which has a more predictable outcome and does not involve feelings of shame and inadequacy. Let's look at the symptoms and causes of the illnesses often confused with depression and see how similar they are to those of depression themselves.

ANAEMIA

There are many different causes for anaemia, which is a blood disorder where haemoglobin, the oxygen-carrying component in red blood cells, is deficient, but the most common one is iron deficiency. Lack of iron can be the result of excessive bleeding from heavy periods, a poor diet, a bleeding stomach ulcer or injury, pregnancy, and less commonly from malabsorption in the gut.

Symptoms: the symptoms of tiredness, pallor, faintness and shortness of breath on exercise are universal with all anaemias. Also brittle nails and skin breakdown, particularly in the sides of the mouth.

Treatment includes blood tests and iron tablets, plus dietary advice.

HYPOTHYROIDISM

Thyroid hormones are essential for body metabolism – i.e. our temperature and how we burn fuel – and the smooth functioning of the nervous system. They also affect sexual function. The thyroid gland can malfunction on two levels, either producing too much of the thyroid hormones, known as hyperthyroidism, or too little, known as hypothyroidism. Hypothyroidism is the thyroid malfunction most commonly associated with depression and has many possible causes.

Symptoms: hypothyroidism causes many of the body's functions to slow down, and can produce symptoms in all parts of the body such as extreme tiredness, weight gain, depression, anxiety, sensitivity to cold, slow heart rate and speech, palpitations, fluid retention, constipation, a hoarse voice, heavy periods, dry, coarse skin, hair thinning or loss, ridged nails. Goitre, a swelling in the front of the neck caused by thyroid gland enlargement, is also a symptom. These symptoms may develop slowly over weeks or months, and it is sometimes difficult to diagnose because of the insidious onset of potential signs. If you have three or more of the above symptoms over a sustained period, then consult your doctor.

Treatment includes thyroid hormone (thyroxine) replacement, or nutritional supplements of iodine.

ADDISON'S DISEASE

This rare disease occurs when the adrenal gland is making too little of the adrenal hormones known as corticosteroids, and as a result the body's metabolism is upset. There are various causes, such as autoimmune disease, where the body attacks its own cells, adrenal cancer and certain drugs.

Symptoms: tiredness and weakness, loss of appetite and weight loss, general feeling of ill health, skin pigmentation like a suntan, particularly in the creases of the palms, knuckles, elbows and knees.

Treatment includes addressing the underlying condition and taking long-term oral corticosteroid drugs.

Contexts for Depression

For some, depression comes about as the result of vulnerability to a particular circumstance, such as seasonal lack of light, hormone changes after childbirth, or a chemical imbalance which promotes manic episodes or schizophrenia.

SEASONAL AFFECTIVE DISORDER (SAD)

One group of depression sufferers it is easier to diagnose is the one in which the depressive illness is triggered by light deprivation during the long hours of darkness in the winter months. None of us likes the lack of light in winter, and we all feel our spirits lift as the spring brings longer days, but for some the problem is a lot more serious. Those affected by SAD become clinically depressed on a seasonal basis. As soon as October (in the northern hemisphere) comes round, these sufferers begin to slide into a downward spiral of depression, and without treatment they will stay depressed till spring.

SAD has many of the same symptoms of other forms of depression, including fatigue, low mood, lethargy, difficulty in waking and carbohydrate craving, the distinguishing mark being the cyclical nature of the depression.

Treating SAD

Luckily for SAD sufferers, light therapy is successful in alleviating depressive symptoms in up to 85 per cent of cases. This therapy requires the person to be exposed, open-eyed, to bright, broad-spectrum light at a mimimum strength of 2500 lux (the unit in which we measure light) for up to two or more hours a day. The light is delivered via a lightbox, and can be used at home or during a visit to a therapist. However, it is important to have your condition diagnosed professionally before using light therapy at home.

POSTNATAL DEPRESSION

Another context for depression is the hormonal flux that affects women after they have given birth. There are three types, the most common being the short-lived emotional disturbance that usually starts between the third to the fifth day after childbirth known as the 'baby blues'. The woman feels tearful and exhausted. It only lasts around two days and seems to be more common among first-time mothers and in those with a history of premenstrual syndrome (PMS).

The next most common is postnatal depression itself, which occurs in around one in five to one in ten mothers and begins within two to three days of childbirth. The symptoms the mother might experience include despondency, tearfulness and irritability, often accompanied by fatigue, anxiety and phobias. She might also have difficulty sleeping, poor concentration, decreased libido and feelings of inadequacy, particularly in relation to her role as a mother. The symptoms may be worse at night, and the depression can last for a few weeks to more than a year. What is particularly distressing about this type of depression is that the bond between the mother and her child is threatened and can affect their relationship in the future.

The third type is a very severe form of depression known as puerperal psychosis and is comparatively rare.

Treating Postnatal Depression

The best scenario in postnatal depression is an early recognition of the condition, so that mother and baby can be given the support that they need. Unfortunately this depressive illness is often put down to the baby blues and no treatment is forthcoming. Treatment has so far been with antidepressants, but Dr Puri's research suggests that EPA is now also a treatment option.

BIPOLAR DISORDER (MANIC DEPRESSION)

This depressive condition combines depression with mania, the two mood states usually occurring in different, distinct phases. To be diagnosed with bipolar disorder, a person needs to have suffered at least one episode of mania. Mania can take various forms, depending on its severity, but during a manic phase a person will experience an elevated mood which is extreme and pathological. They often speak very loudly and quickly and won't stop, jumping from one subject to another without apparent connection, as if they had been 'fast-forwarded'. They can become delusional, believing things that are not true and acting on this belief, so that, for instance, they might spend huge amounts of money they don't have, or think that they are God. Their perceptions can change, so they might fail to notice that they have injured themselves, or that they are not eating and drinking adequately. They can act completely out of character, often engaging in highly flirtatious behaviour and sexual promiscuity. They might also suffer hallucinations. And they believe all the while that their behaviour is normal.

In general, patients with bipolar disorder have a history of mood swings, with episodes of both mania and depression. But they are diagnosed with the condition as soon as a manic phase has been identified, even if a depressive episode has not yet occurred.

Treating Bipolar Disorder

The most common treatment for manic depression is a long-term maintenance course of the drugs lithium carbonate and carbamazepine, although it is not clear how these drugs work to reduce the symptoms, and both drugs have potentially troublesome side effects. A common problem with manic-depressive patients is keeping them on their medication long term, as they can reach a stage where they believe they no longer need the drugs. However, EPA and high EPA essential fatty acid supplements appear to have mood-stabilising properties which make them potentially therapeutic in bipolar disorder.

SCHIZOPHRENIA

This disease is strongly associated with clinical depression, meaning that schizophrenics also commonly suffer the symptoms of depression. Schizophrenia is often first manifest in teenage years, which makes for problems in diagnosis as normal teenage moods can seem quite severe and alienated. Symptoms of the disease are many and varied, and, like depressive symptoms, can also vary in number and intensity and have a genetic component. In its mildest form, the exceptional thought patterns can push boundaries in art and science. They might include: an increasing need for solitude; a lack of response to those close to the sufferer, or a cold, blank response; disrupted sleep patterns where the sufferer can end up sleeping during the day and staying awake all night; bizarre thought patterns and connections which confuse both themselves and others; agitation and restlessness; delusions and paranioa, where they come to believe that they are the victim of hostile forces which are trying to control and persecute them; hallucinations, where the schizophrenic hears voices, sometimes commanding them to perform totally irrational and often destructive tasks; general hostility to those close to them.

An interesting feature of the disease is that its distribution worldwide is absolutely consistent. All populations have the same level of incidence, between 0.5 and 1.5 per cent over a lifetime. Culture, race, social circumstances and so on make no difference. This is not true of any other illness. However, once the disease had developed, the countries whose diet had a high intake of saturated fat – which is thought to be destructive to essential fatty acids and therefore the production of EPA – had worse results in controlling the course of the disease than the countries whose diet contained little saturated fat.

Treating Schizophrenia

Schizophrenia can be difficult to treat successfully over the long term. Antipsychotic drugs such as chloropromazine, which control symptoms of hallucination and help to stabilise mood, are the main treatment option, combined with general support in dealing with the disease.

However, schizophrenia is the disease which is in the forefront of the research done by David Horrobin, Krishna Vaddadi, Malcolm Peet, Basant Puri, Jan Mellor and Alex Richardson, which has led to the discovery of EPA as a treatment for depression. Their studies have also shown that a high-dose EPA supplement alleviates the symptoms of schizophrenia considerably, with none of the unpleasant side effects that have traditionally plagued the long-term users of antipsychotic drugs.

Warning: if you are currently taking antipsychotic drugs, do not stop taking them without first consulting your doctor, who will advise a gradual reduction of dose.

If there is a particular context for your depression, such as one of those mentioned above, it is important that it is recognised, not only so that the appropriate treatment can be started and help given, but so that you can be aware of your possible vulnerability to the illness in the future. For instance, if you are diagnosed with SAD, you will know that the approach of winter is a time to be starting light therapy and making sure your levels of EPA are high.

What Happens if Depression Goes Untreated?

This obviously depends on the nature and severity of your depressive episode, but it is a fact that a large number of depression sufferers just fight it out by themselves with no professional help. This can have disastrous consequences if the person becomes suicidal, not to mention the fact that a prolonged, undiagnosed bout of depression can wreak havoc with families and career prospects. Where a boss might be sympathetic to an employee taking time off to be treated for depression, they might not look so favourably on a person whose concentration, people skills, speed and efficiency suddenly deteriorate for no apparent reason. And someone living with a depressed spouse will find it a lot easier to be tolerant and sympathetic if they feel their partner is taking the appropriate steps to speed recovery. This is why it is so important to diagnose and treat the condition as soon as possible.

Depression, however, is not necessarily progressive. You may experience a mild or moderate episode which remains just that, mild or moderate, regardless of whether it is treated or not.

Problems Accessing Help

One of the snags in getting treatment is that a depressed person finds it particularly difficult to access the help that is offered, or even find the motivation to take the antidepressant medication.

One of the side effects of depressive illness is that when someone tries to help a depressed person – perhaps talking to them, hugging them, generally caring for them – the depressed person can see the help is being offered, but somehow cannot take comfort from it. The kind words mean nothing, the embrace doesn't soothe, in fact often exactly the opposite: the help only makes you irritable, and guilty at your lack of responsiveness.

Who Gets Depressed?

No one knows exactly why, but some of us are more vulnerable to depression than others. Even with reactive depression, where a person is depressed following a life trauma, another person might experience the same trauma and not get depressive symptoms. They might be sad and miserable for a while, and go through a normal phase of reaction to the event, but it will not be followed by depression. And a person who does experience reactive depression after one upsetting event might not do so when faced with another equally distressing circumstance.

There have been many theories put forward by doctors and scientists over the years in an attempt to explain this complex disease, covering biological, psychological and social factors. And it is thought that often a person's depressive illness is triggered by a combination of these factors rather than one particular villain.

Professor Horrobin's research, followed up by Dr Puri and his colleagues, sheds more light on what might be a large factor at the root of mental illness, indicating that depression might have a mainly biological genesis, specifically the lack of EPA in our diet. However, there is still the fact that gender, age, our genetic inheritance, and marital and social status have so far been highlighted in statistics as playing a significant role in depression too.

WOMEN AT RISK

Women, it appears, are two to three times more likely to suffer from a major depressive episode than are men. Is this to do with women's hormonal make-up? If so, there is as yet no research to back up this theory. Given that women tend to eat roughly the same food as men and live in the same environment, why should they be more susceptible? Married men, for instance, have lower rates of depression than single men, but married women are no better off than single, widowed or divorced women when it comes to depression. There have been various hypotheses – some rather improbable – bandied about concerning women's increased vulnerability, such as the idea that women are more likely to have been sexually abused as children, again not backed up by research. Or that modern women have a more stressful, more complicated life trying to raise families, run homes and have full-time careers, and that many are failing to cope. Or the theory that women are more sensitive than men, making them more likely to react badly to trauma and sadness.

The Depression Alliance, a mental health charity, suggests that men and women may in fact suffer the same amount of depressive illness, it's just that women are twice as likely to seek help and be diagnosed as their male counterparts. They also suggest that doctors, faced with a man complaining of depressive symptoms, are less likely to diagnose them with depression than if the patient were a woman.

However, the truth is that we just do not know which of these possibilities is the most likely contributor to the higher incidence of depression in women.

TEENAGE AND YOUNG ADULT MALES AT RISK

Young adult males, you might think, given their high rate of suicide – the highest, certainly, of any group – are more prone to depression than their girlfriends. In fact, post-puberty, they are less likely to suffer a depressive episode.

The discrepancy is partly explained by the methods of suicide that young men tend to choose. Young women most commonly opt for pills, which are less predictable in outcome, whereas boys go for the more violent and unfortunately more successful methods.

But there is still the alarming 85 per cent increase in young male suicides over a recent ten-year period to be explained. Are they also finding the pressures of the modern world too difficult to cope with? Or, with illicit drugs and alcohol increasingly available to young people, are they more likely to succumb than their girlfriends, making them vulnerable to violent mood swings and endangering behaviour? Again, we don't know.

OLDER PEOPLE AT RISK

Old people are particularly vulnerable to depression. Research in the US suggests as many as one in twelve Americans aged sixty-five or over are suffering from major depression, although it seems their symptoms often go unrecognised. You might think it reasonable that old people, particularly if they are lonely, ill or in care, might suffer from an increased incidence of depression. And much of this increase may be explained by the prevalence of diseases in the elderly that are associated with depression, such as dementia, stroke and Parkinson's. Also, old people are twice as likely to be on medication, some of which is linked to symptoms of depressive illness, such as some beta-blockers used to lower blood pressure. But it is still important that the disease is recognised so that they can receive appropriate treatment to alleviate their symptoms. Or perhaps take preventative measures in the form of a daily EPA supplement (see Chapter 5).

GENETIC INHERITANCE

There is good evidence that a genetic factor plays a role for some people who suffer from clinical depression. One route the research scientists have taken is to look at whether or not a depressed person has a first-degree relative who has suffered from the disease. Unfortunately, a study that follows this route has also to take into account the 'nature versus nurture' component. For example, a parent who is suffering from a depressive illness while raising their child might treat the child differently to the way in which a non-sufferer relates to their offspring.

Twin Research

A better way of studying genetic factors is to examine twins. We know that identical twins share the same DNA; the genetic code in their chromosomes is identical. In contrast, non-identical twins share on average only 50 per cent of their genetic material. But of course twins, whether they are identical or not, will receive roughly the same parenting and the same environmental messages, from diet, schooling, economic and social factors.

A study of this kind will first have to find pairs of twins, both identical and non-identical, in which one twin has become depressed. It then needs to establish whether, and if so how often, the other twin in the pair also suffers a depressive episode. If genetic factors are important, then the study would expect to find that the identical twins had a higher incidence of both twins suffering depressive episodes than the non-identical.

A 1996 study into depressive illness at the University of Wales College of Medicine in Cardiff studied 177 pairs of British twins where at least one twin had a diagnosis of major depression according to the American DSM-IV criteria. They found that the incidence of both twins suffering a major depressive illness ran at 20 per cent in the non-identical twins, but in the identical twins that rate was more than doubled at 46 per cent. This is strong evidence that there is a genetic component in the causation of depression.

So far, however, no specific 'depressive gene' has been identified. Scientists working in this burgeoning field of research believe that there are perhaps a number of genes responsible, not just one, and that they act together to produce depressive illness. But until a gene or genes is identified, no one will understand how exactly they change the person's brain patterns to create depression.

The fact that there is a genetic component in depressive illness does not mean that if you have a close relative who suffers from depression you will automatically become depressed. As we have said earlier, genetics are just one of the factors that are now seen to be linked to depression. But when scientists finally crack the disease's genetic identity, it will tell us a great deal more about the origins of depression and why one person suffers and not another.

SOCIAL DEPRIVATION

Social deprivation has long been thought to be a precipitating factor in depressive illness. If you live with the stress of unemployment or low-paid work where you are not properly valued, the humiliation of benefits, and the worry about whether you will have enough money to pay the bills and feed the children, it is hardly surprising that you might be more vulnerable to depressive symptoms than your more well-off counterparts. However, as with all depression factors, it isn't as simple as 'If you're deprived you're depressed.' There is debate about the statistics that show that people suffering socioeconomic deprivation have a higher rate of depressive illness, some experts saying that severe depression naturally inclines a person to drift into poverty, as they can no longer hold down a job or relationships. The other side of the argument is that the stress of poverty causes depression, combined with the likelihood that a person who has a miserable life is more vulnerable to the abuse of alcohol and illicit drugs, which in themselves can promote depressive symptoms.

A recent study at Cornell University in America linked inadequate food intake and a poor diet with depression, which supports Professor Horrobin and Dr Puri's contention that a brain starved of sufficient fatty acids is vulnerable to mental illness. The study found that 60 per cent of adolescents who lived with inadequate food intake had at least one suicidal symptom – i.e. they had considered committing suicide – and 20 per cent had attempted suicide.

Whether it's chicken or egg, there is a significant link between social deprivation and depression, but, again, just because you are poor does not mean you will necessarily suffer from the symptoms of depression.

RICH PEOPLE GET DEPRESSED TOO

Although we have mentioned groups of people who might be more vulnerable to depression, that does not mean that depression only strikes these groups. Anyone can get depressed, even celebrities, eminent scientists, politicians, writers, artists and people who have, to the casual observer, the most perfect lives. Winston Churchill, a famous depressive, called his depression 'Black Dog'. Other well-known sufferers include Van Gogh, Ernest Hemingway, Marx and Caroline Aherne. No category of person is immune, and although a person who has once suffered a major depression will possibly fall victim to another bout, equally they may not. And now, with the new discovery about the brain-supporting properties of EPA, there is the real chance that those who have been prone to depression in the past can take a daily supplement of EPA to ward off any further attacks.

Are YOU Depressed?

We have listed some of the types who might be particularly vulnerable to depression, but it is important to remember that anyone can fall prey to the illness, not just the ones mentioned above. You might recognise a trigger for your symptoms in the categories above, but equally you might not fall into any of these groups, yet you are still experiencing what feels like depression.

With so many cases of depression unrecognised and therefore untreated, you may be one of those suffering depressive symptoms but still wondering what exactly is wrong with you. You may feel foolish bothering the doctor, worried they will think you are wasting their time and convinced all they will say is, 'Pull yourself together.' But not knowing what the matter is can be unnecessarily frightening, and obviously the sooner you know the reason for your symptoms, the sooner you can get treatment. Use the questions listed below as a quick guide to how you might be feeling if you are suffering a depressive episode:

- Has your mood changed over the past few weeks from your normal, day-to-day pattern to become more pessimistic and dark? This does not mean just having a bad day, it means a more sustained lowering of mood. Some people are naturally quieter and more introverted than others, but it is the change you should be looking for.

- Are you feeling hopeless about life for no particular reason? Obviously if you have just suffered a personal tragedy, or even a less major emotional trauma, you will not be feeling full of the joys of spring, but this is a generalised despair about everything around you which is not justified by the actual circumstances in your life.
- Are you exhausted? Again, this is not the normal tiredness you might feel after a busy day, or a period of high stress; this is a more fundamental tiredness, a deep bone-tiredness which seems to settle over your mind and body and make you feel incapable of even the smallest effort.
- Do you find nothing makes you smile any more? Not even the prospect of a holiday, a new dress, or seeing your favourite friend for a drink? Do you find yourself constantly making feeble excuses to get yourself out of work and social engagements?
- Are you having trouble sleeping? Do you wake up horribly early in the morning and lie there feeling exhausted and miserable at the prospect of another day?
- Are you feeling ashamed of your low mood and think it is all your fault?
- Have you experienced panic attacks or feelings of high anxiety about everyday situations you would normally find easy to deal with? For instance, going out, meeting friends, taking a meeting at work, going down a high escalator, driving.
- Are you finding it's hard to concentrate, are you having difficulty getting through your daily tasks, is it impossible to make decisions?
- Have some of your family or friends begun asking you what is the matter? Do you get angry and irritated when they do?

- When people try and cheer you up, do their efforts fail to comfort you and seem utterly pointless?
- Do you spend a lot of your day with negative, despairing thoughts churning about in your brain?
- Have you started drinking or smoking an abnormal amount?
- Do you just want to give up? Does everything seems too difficult and you simply haven't the energy to cope any more?

If you have answered 'yes' to three or more of these questions, you should go and see your doctor because you are showing the classic symptoms of depressive illness. Write a list of the symptoms you are experiencing before you go, so that you can give them a clear picture of your problem. It is easy to forget what you meant to say when GP consultations are so short, particularly as you are finding it difficult to think straight. If your doctor doesn't listen or understand, make an appointment with a different doctor, and take a friend along to back you up. It's important to get a diagnosis for your symptoms, and eliminate other medical conditions, so that you can begin treatment.

Being Close to Depression

The person suffering from depression is not the only one who is affected by this disease. Everyone who comes into contact with someone who is even moderately depressed will feel the impact. There are three main problems to consider in coping with a person, either at work or at home, who is in the throes of a depressive illness: recognising the problem, understanding the problem, helping them to get treatment.

RECOGNISING THE PROBLEM

First we have to recognise that the person in question is depressed. This, as we have already discussed, is not easy. But it might be easier for you to spot it in someone else than it is for the sufferer themself to identify their problem. This is because their perceptions will be clouded, their normal reality distorted. If you notice a marked and prolonged mood change in someone close to you, which may be accompanied by general tiredness and lack of enthusiasm, negative thinking, disturbed sleep and eating patterns, perhaps an increase in alcohol consumption and loss of libido, then you should consider depression as the cause.

Because of their distorted perceptions, they may resist any suggestion of depression as a diagnosis for their mood disruption. They will be trying valiantly to be 'normal' again, and may feel ashamed of the way they are feeling and behaving, particularly if they are harbouring suicidal thoughts. They will be hoping that it will pass, that tomorrow they will wake up and feel different.

UNDERSTANDING THE PROBLEM

There are a few facts that are important to understand when you are trying to cope with a person in a depressed state:
- You cannot cheer up someone who is experiencing a serious depressive episode.
- The depression sufferer cannot cheer themselves up, nor can they 'snap out of it'.
- They cannot take in what you say or react usefully to your help and advice in the way they normally would.
- Their depression is not your fault and hardly ever even related to you.

- Likewise, there is no shame or blame attached to being depressed. You can contract depression like any other illness, such as cancer or heart disease.
- Teenagers and children can also experience depression.
- Depressed people are more likely to be a danger to themselves than to anyone else.
- There are very successful treatments for alleviating the symptoms of depression. And now, with EPA, they do not involve side effects.

It is vital that you, as a person close to depression, understand these facts, because a lot of the anguish surrounding the disease is caused by frustration engendered by misunderstanding. There is no doubt that dealing with a depressed person who is not responding, whose behaviour is strange and erratic and who is refusing to seek help is frustrating and extremely daunting. The subsequent impact on relationships, both at home and at work, if depression goes unrecognised can be devastating.

HELPING THEM TO GET TREATMENT

So you have recognised that someone close to you is depressed, but either they won't admit to it, or they admit it but are adamant that they don't want treatment. What do you do? The answer depends very much on the degree of severity of the depressive symptoms. Unless they are very severely affected, it should be possible to talk to them about seeing a doctor. They may not respond at once, but keep trying, or get someone else close to them to try. Let them know that you understand how they are feeling, and that they have your full support. Nagging won't work. If it is a work colleague affected, contact a close friend or family member and tell them your concerns. If they continue to refuse to get medical help, see their GP yourself and ask them to drop round and talk to the person about their symptoms.

Depression in children and teenagers is notoriously difficult to spot, not least because you don't expect them to get the illness so young. And how are you supposed to tell the difference between a normally sulky, monosyllabic teenager who refuses to eat what you cook or get out of bed or function in a way that you consider appropriate, and a depressed teenager? The answer is that often you can't, but signs to look for are marked changes in mood, within the context of teenager behaviour. For instance, a stroppy teenager who has lots of friends, and then suddenly becomes lethargic and has no interest in seeing their mates. Or a teenager who begins to drink excessively and regularly. Or a teenager who seems to get absolutely no pleasure from a treat, such as some extra money for clothes. If you think someone you know is in danger of harming themselves, you must seek help immediately by contacting their GP and explaining the problem. Don't rely on the problem going away. Someone intent on suicide will find a way, and you are not responsible for their actions; but a person may still be at the stage where they are just desperate and confused.

Don't forget, this is a difficult illness and there are no hard and fast rules to play by. But understanding is certainly the key.

Points to Remember

- Depression is an illness just as cancer and heart disease are illnesses.

- Two-thirds of those suffering a serious depressive episode do not seek professional help. This is because there is still a strong stigma attached to depression. Many sufferers, and the people close to them, feel ashamed of their condition, thinking it shows mental and emotional weakness.

- Depression is not just a normal low mood which the sufferer can 'snap out of' by 'pulling themselves together'.

- Depression is now classified as mild, moderate or severe, with diagnosis relying on the number and severity of symptoms present over a period of two weeks or more. The key identifying symptom present in all people suffering from depression is an overwhelming feeling of hopelessness and despair which will not go away.

- Diagnosis is hampered by the fact that depression sufferers can have such a variety and degree of symptoms that it can be hard for the doctor to pinpoint. Depression can sometimes be confused with other illnesses. Sufferers might find it difficult to articulate their problem clearly.

- Depression can have several different associated contexts. These include seasonal affective disorder (SAD), postnatal depression, bipolar disorder (manic depression) and schizophrenia.

- Groups most frequently affected by depressive illness include women, older people, those with a family history of depression and those who are socially and economically deprived.

- No one is guaranteed immunity from depression.

- Those close to a person suffering from depression need information and support to cope with the problem too.

- EPA offers an alternative, side-effect-free treatment to antidepressant and antipsychotic drugs for depression and related mental disorders.

Chapter Three

Why Do We Get Depressed?

It seems from ancient texts that human beings have always suffered from depression. Saul, it appears, suffered a bout of it when the Philistines were being uppity and he had lost his faith in God; and Hippocrates, the famous ancient Greek physician who is considered to be the father of medicine, described what he called 'melancholia' in the same terms as modern-day depression. Yet even after thousands of years the definitive cause of depression is still something of a mystery to scientific researchers worldwide. There does seem to be agreement on the fact that there is no single cause for depression, but rather a number of contributory factors which come together and trigger a depressive episode in people who are vulnerable. This consensus is only a jumping-off point, however, because no one is sure which combination of factors is needed, or why one person reacts to one set of contributory factors and another does not. And it is even true that a person who is vulnerable one time might not be so vulnerable the next. So unfortunately there is no single formula that states A+B+C=depression, as, for instance, you have in equation low immune system + flu virus = bout of flu. It is best to think of depression as a cake, and the factors that contribute to it are the ingredients. There are many different methods and many different ingredients that can be used to make a cake. The tiniest inconsistency in temperature or ingredients can change the outcome. Not to mention the fact that you can make it exactly the same way twice and get a totally different result.

Even if there is no simple formula, there is still a lot you can learn about the roots of your depressive symptoms. Depression ingredients include various biological, psychological, physical and social factors, and this chapter outlines all these factors in detail, and also describes how they might interact with each other, so that you have a clearer idea about how you might have become vulnerable to this disease. But remember, no one factor can be said to cause depression every time and in every case. If this were true, then, say, everyone who was socially deprived would be expected to contract depressive symptoms, and this is certainly not the case.

The good news is that most of these depression triggers are open to change. For instance, if your life reflects psychological factors such as childhood neglect and negative thinking, then you can find help in facing up to these problems and so reduce the number of factors in your life that might make you prone to depression in the future. Or if stress is a contributory factor you can identify what is causing you to be so stressed and go about modifying these elements. Or if low levels of EPA are a factor – which Basant Puri has shown them to be – then you can increase your EPA levels and help alleviate your depression.

We explain this biological factor – Basant Puri's fatty acid theory about low levels of EPA in the brain – in detail in this chapter; it is one that he believes is crucial in triggering depressive illness, and which challenges the current thinking about the biochemistry of depression. We go back millions of years to the beginnings of human brain development, and chart the EPA theory through the years of research and trials to the point Dr Puri has now reached, where he can put it into practical application in the treatment of depression.

So to answer the question 'Why do we get depressed?' let's first look at the various contributory factors and see to what extent your life might reflect these elements.

The Contributory Factors in Depression

PSYCHOLOGICAL FACTORS

There have been a host of different theories put forward by psychologists and psychoanalysts over the years to help to explain the mindset that is present in many depressed people. They are theories that address the way we think and feel about ourselves and others in the light of our experiences. Many psychologists believe that these experiences, usually unhappy or traumatic, happened in childhood, and have set a blueprint for our thought patterns and reactions to those around us for the rest of our lives. You may recognise these theories in relation to your own life.

Loss

Loss is a recurring theme in psychoanalytic theory. You may have experienced loss in your childhood. This does not mean losing a material object, but rather the loss of proper emotional support when you were a child and most vulnerable; for instance not being nurtured properly by your mother. The psychoanalysts believe that if you did not have this reliable support when you needed it, you can find it hard to make successful relationships with others later in life, and you may become prone to depression as a result. It is not always easy to know how we were looked after when we were small, but you might remember not feeling predominantly safe and happy, or being frightened, neglected or criticised by the person caring for you. This sort of treatment might leave you with the feeling that you are not a person worthy of love and respect.

Helplessness

This is another strand to this same theme of loss. Perhaps you were brought up by a mother who, for whatever reason, was not able to make you feel safe and loved, but, being a child, you had no control over the way you were treated. Some psychoanalysts believe that you will react to this unhappiness by giving up and becoming passive and withdrawn. You feel there is nothing you can do to change things, and no point in struggling against what you have found to be the way of the world.

Then if, as an adult, you are faced with a similar feeling of helplessness and grief, such as when someone close to you dies, or your spouse leaves you, or you lose your job, then you react in a similar way, believing that all action is futile, and you withdraw into depression. This mindset can also be brought about by the death of a parent when you were young, especially if the death was never properly discussed and explained.

Lack of Positive Reinforcement

This is a theory that addresses how you were treated in childhood too. Perhaps the people close to you never praised you or made you feel that there was anything to look forward to. If this was the case, you might eventually just give up and stop bothering to make any effort, and again become vulnerable to a depressive episode. Maybe every time you attempted something, like painting a picture at school, your mother would laugh at it, or ignore it, or tease you about it. Perhaps your efforts to learn to swim were ridiculed, or your ability to make friends was mocked. You can see how after a while you, as a child, would just stop bothering. You might then unconsciously carry that same pattern into adulthood, making you negative, lacking in ambition, unable to experience pleasure, and therefore vulnerable to depression.

Negative Thought Patterns

These are key to the theory of the cognitive psychologists, who believe that it is the way you *think* about yourself and your environment, more than what is actually going on in your life, that affects your happiness and the likelihood of you developing depression. They developed what they call the 'cognitive triad', which is made up of three fundamental mind-sets. Look at these statements and see if they relate to the way you see the world.

- You have a negative view of yourself; i.e. you have low self-esteem.
- You have a negative view of events that occur in relation to yourself; i.e. you always think the world is against you, even if this has no bearing on the truth.
- You have a negative view of the future; i.e. you don't believe it will ever get any better, something will always go wrong.

Is this how you think? If you do, then the cognitive therapists believe you could be the victim of inadequate nurturing when you were a child. Perhaps your mother or father constantly told you that you were stupid, clumsy, lazy, ugly, generally unlovable, and you believed them. Now you have absorbed this distorted information and it colours everything you do and the way you deal with everyone you come in contact with as an adult. So you are always waiting for the insult, you then overreact and treat your friends and acquaintances with paranoia and suspicion, which in turn alienates them, and this distorted thought pattern becomes a self-fulfilling prophecy, because people then don't find you lovable. The end result? Depression again.

Trying Too Hard to Be Good and Perfect

Doing this because you believe that you are intrinsically worthless and bad is another mindset that can lead to depression. Trying to be perfect is inevitably doomed to failure, no matter who you are, but many of us do this in an attempt to negate the horrible feelings we have about ourselves inside. So perhaps you are always charming and helpful and there for everyone, always the one who does the extra school run or takes the difficult project, makes all the costumes for the school play and gives everyone presents for no reason. Nothing wrong with that, you might say, and no, there isn't, except if you are doing it in a desperate attempt to be what you consider a 'good' person because your childhood carers have instilled in you how bad you really are. This 'trying to be good' mindset is a terrible strain and will often lead in the end to depression.

These different mindsets identified by psychoanalytic theory can be very hard to live with, not least because so many of us are unaware that we think and feel this way. You might know that you don't feel good about yourself, but it is another leap to understand why you feel this way or how it is affecting your life. If you think that there are issues here that you relate to, it may be a good idea to get professional help from a qualified therapist (see Chapter 6), because our internal messages about ourselves and others seem to be of prime importance in mood disorders such as depression.

The theories all point to our childhood blueprint as key to the way we feel about ourselves. A perfect childhood may be something of a myth, but the majority of us received nurturing that was good enough. Psychological research suggests that for the rest of us, however, it is the lack of proper safety and respect during childhood that might tip us towards depression in adult life.

BIOLOGICAL FACTORS

As well as the psychological factors in depression, there are also factors that relate to the actual make-up of the tissues in the body. These are the brain chemicals, hormones and genes, and a disruption of the body's norm in any of these elements is thought to contribute to depressive illness. It is not always clear why these elements are disrupted, although modern diet and lifestyle are thought to contribute (see Chapter 6), but righting the balance of these chemicals has been the main function of antidepressant treatment over the last few decades. Dr Puri's fatty acid theory is based on depression having a strong biological component, and we discuss this later in the chapter. The problem for a depression sufferer is that there is no warning that our body chemicals are out of kilter before we become depressed.

Why Do We Get Depressed?

Body Chemicals

Low levels of EPA are associated with depression, but there are other chemicals in our bodies, amino acids – the biochemical compounds that make up proteins – which are key in the production of the mood-enhancing brain chemicals serotonin and noradrenaline. Low levels of these brain chemicals, also known as neurotransmitters, have been strongly linked to depression. Like essential fatty acids, eight of these amino acids are called 'essential amino acids', and are vital for healthy body function. Two, called l-phenylalanine and l-tryptophan, are needed for the production of serotonin and noradrenaline. Your body does not make these amino acids, so you have to get them from food, such as milk products, bananas, chicken, fish, meat, peanuts and sesame seeds. Why one person has low levels of these neurotransmitters and not another is still a mystery, and whether the low levels actually cause depression, or whether depression causes the low levels, is still up for debate. However, Basant Puri's fatty acid theory goes a long way to explain how these low levels of neurotransmitters occur in a brain that is not functioning properly because of a lack of EFAs. If you support your brain, your neurotransmitter levels should right themselves.

Genes

We have discussed how depression has a genetic component, but there is another interesting aspect to the gene debate: that of depression as a survival mechanism. Charles Darwin's theory that it is only the fittest genes that survive suggests that if the depression gene is hereditary, then perhaps it has some survival value. This may sound odd, since the common perception of depression is that it increases the likelihood of early death, not that it helps the race survive.

However, studies with apes have shown that depressive behaviour, which is by nature passive and withdrawn, could be a survival mechanism against a superior opponent, as the ape exhibiting this type of behaviour appears to be non-aggressive and therefore not threatening. You might think that passive behaviour has no place in our intensely competitive modern world, but it is possible that we still unconsciously use depression as a means of withdrawing from a world we are finding hard to cope with, and that this withdrawal is our attempt at survival.

SOCIAL FACTORS

Social factors figure strongly in contributing to depression, which makes sense as we are powerfully influenced by the environment, both physical and social, in which we live. You can't help but be upset by a particular circumstance, such as someone close to you dying, or you and your partner separating or getting a divorce, or losing your job. When something traumatic like this happens to you, obviously you react. Sometimes you will go through the grieving process and carry on with your life as usual, sometimes you will get angry and be galvanised to change an aspect of your life as a result; for instance you might get a new job which you had never thought to apply for when you were in steady employment, but which you infinitely prefer. And sometimes you react by becoming depressed. This is known as reactive depression, and is not thought to have a biological component.

There are also other less specific, wider social issues that are thought to be contributory factors, which include general life stresses such as ongoing poverty, loneliness and unwelcome change. But don't forget that most medical professionals believe that depression is a result of many different factors coming together. So, looking at your own life, what social factors should you watch out for as possibly contributing to your depressive illness?

Let's take two women, Woman A and Woman B. Both women's husbands have just died.

Woman A's profile: she has high levels of essential fatty acids obtained through a healthy diet. She has been brought up in a nurturing family. She has a secure job. She is not in the habit of drinking or smoking to excess. She has no family history of depression.

Woman B's profile: she eats a poor diet, low in EFAs and high in saturated fats. She suffers from very low self-esteem because she was not properly nurtured as a child. She doesn't work and worries about money. She smokes a lot, regularly drinks large amounts of alcohol and takes recreational drugs. Her father suffered from frequent bouts of depressive illness.

Woman A, although she is devastated about losing her husband, is more likely to be able to grieve appropriately and cope with her tragedy. She will experience many mood swings in the weeks following his death, including sadness, anger, numbness and disbelief, but the moods will eventually pass into acceptance.

Woman B, however, is statistically much more likely to succumb to a depressive episode. But it is not just the fact of her husband dying that can be blamed for Woman B's depression. She might have succumbed to the illness without her husband's death. That perhaps tipped her into depression, but she was already susceptible from the accumulation of the other biological, psychological and social factors.

It should also be mentioned that, given depression is such a complex, unpredictable disease, it might well happen that neither woman, or both, will experience depression, despite the probabilities. So when you look at the list of contributory social factors, don't panic and assume that if you are currently experiencing one you will necessarily fall into a depression.

Loss

We have discussed how loss in early childhood changes the way we think and feel about ourselves, but loss is also a reality for everyone. We all experience loss at some time in our life, and so it acts as a social, reactive trigger for depression, as Woman A and Woman B illustrated. The problem is that we all try to attach permanence to our surroundings – the relationships, work and material possessions that lend structure to our lives – because these structures give us a sense of security. Although we know logically that nothing is permanent, and that any event can occur at any time to reduce all we have to nothing, most of us still cling to the illusion of permanence. And so when something happens to shatter that illusion, and we lose something dear to us, we can be very badly affected. What can then compound the problem is that you feel you should be able to cope with what has happened, but often you just can't.

Here are some of the loss events that might trigger a reactive bout of depression. Some, as you see, are not necessarily serious, but if they hit you at the wrong place or the wrong time, they can feel very serious:

- You lose your partner, either to death or divorce.
- You lose your health and mobility.
- You lose a best friend, either through death, argument or geography.

64

- You lose a parent. Even if your parent is old and their death appropriate, this doesn't necessarily make the event any less painful.
- You lose a beloved pet.
- You lose your material wealth.
- You lose your home and community, perhaps relocating to an area where you know no one.
- You lose your faith.

Whatever the loss, it is not only painful in itself, but it can also highlight other aspects of your life that in happier times you could manage to ignore. For instance, your husband leaves you, and this exposes all your long-held insecurities about being unlovable, dating back a lifetime. Or your mother dies and you finally have to face up to the fact that you had a terrible relationship with her. The combination of these powerful emotions can often send a vulnerable person into a depression.

Repressed feelings

How we deal with a loss event is as important to our depression as the event itself. Unfortunately, we in the West are not good at dealing with loss. Many communities have forgotten the supportive rituals surrounding death, and increased mobility for economic reasons has meant that we are often not living close to family and friends who in the past might have offered consolation.

If we are not able to express our grief at some traumatic event, we can turn this sadness inwards where it festers and can re-emerge as depressive symptoms. But it is not always easy to say how we are feeling, especially if your friends and family seem embarrassed by your grief. Here are a few tips to help you deal with a loss:

- Cry if you want to. Crying is a vital body function for dealing with strong emotion, as scratching deals with an itch. You should never be ashamed of showing emotion.
- Be honest about how you feel, both to yourself and others. It is not always appropriate to go into detail, but don't always say you are fine when you are not.
- Find someone, or a few people, who is prepared to let you talk about what has happened to you. If your friends are unhelpful, try a bereavement counsellor.
- Don't be hustled out of your grief. You are entitled to feel sad for as long as you like. Obviously it is easier for those close to you if you get over your grief as quickly as possible, but it is not helpful to you. Experts say that it takes at least two years to go through the grief of a partner's death.
- Be kind to yourself if you are experiencing a loss. Don't try to carry on as normal. If you want to cancel social engagements or avoid extra work pressures, then do so.
- Try not to use alcohol or recreational drugs in excess to dull the pain of your grief. It may seem to help in the short term, but it can make you feel worse in the long run.
- Whatever you do, don't bottle up your unhappiness.

Isolation

It is hard to understand how, in a world that seems to be exploding with people, modern Western society creates so much isolation. But many of us experience feelings of loneliness and isolation even within our family structure. There are many reasons why people have become isolated:

- Economic migration. Living as we used to in small towns and villages, everyone knew everyone else, and families lived alongside each other. This is not to say that the old social structure didn't have its own stresses and strains, but at least you knew your neighbours and you probably worked with them too. People looked out for each other, and this is very important when you are old, ill, or a lonely young mother stuck at home all day with a grizzling baby.

- Economic independence can, perversely, be another isolating factor. The number of people, particularly women, living alone has soared in the last twenty years, and one of the reasons is that they can afford to do so. This is not to say that living alone causes depression, it doesn't, but if you are prone to depression, being alone too much can exacerbate any tendency to introversion and low mood, and also separate you from avenues of help.
- Divorce – for both the parents and the children. Children, particularly in stepfamilies, often suffer real isolation if they don't fit into the new family structure.
- Children leaving home.
- Spiritual isolation is on the increase. We live in a secular society, with only 3 per cent of Britons attending church regularly, and this can leave us feeling as if there is no larger context to our lives, no purpose beyond the pursuit of material comforts. Lack of faith also means that if we are feeling down about something, we have no spiritual counsellor to whom we can turn for help and guidance.

Being alone is not the same as being lonely. You need time on your own, when you can wind down and not have to think about others, but enforced isolation can be mentally wearing. If you do feel isolated, remember that there are many others out there who feel the same way, and therefore many avenues for improving your life so that you do not feel so alone. Nowadays dating agencies have lost their stigma, with the Internet providing an easy way of contacting others, but if you are not ready to meet new people on a one-to-one basis, why not join a class, such as an exercise, dance, art, cooking, writing or gardening class. You don't even have to say anything at first, but being with people who are enjoying the same thing as you will automatically create a bond.

Coping with Change

Change is good, change is challenging. We all need change to stimulate us and progress our lives, otherwise we risk getting stuck in a boring life routine. However, how you react to change is key to whether it becomes a positive or a negative experience. Answer these questions to see how good you are at coping with change:

- Do you have a fixed routine to your life?
- Do you hate changes in this routine? For instance, it upsets you if the café you usually have coffee in has closed for the day, or the supermarket has moved the items you normally buy to another aisle.
- Do you get flustered if someone asks you to do something on the spur of the moment?
- Have you got the same friends you've had for years, with no new ones?
- Do you rely on other people to do the same thing at the same time, just as you do, and get upset when they are unreliable?
- Do you worry about things changing around you, for instance the local cinema becoming a leisure centre?
- Do you worry that you won't be able to cope if things change?

If you have answered 'yes' to the majority of these questions, then change is obviously difficult for you, and makes you anxious, perhaps raising questions of inadequacy. You have regulated your life as much as you can to create a feeling of security, but you might be very vulnerable if this routine were upset. Try to introduce an element of change, however small, into your daily life. Walk a different way to the Tube, buy a new variety of fruit, make a new friend, try a different newspaper. When you know you can cope with small changes, the bigger ones become less threatening.

Addiction and Depression

The relationship between addiction to alcohol and drugs and depression is a complex one. Studies have shown, for instance, that people suffering from depression are about twice as likely to be alcohol-dependent – i.e. if you don't consume a regular supply of alcohol you suffer from symptoms of withdrawal – than the rest of the population. This, again, does not mean that alcohol or drug abuse causes depression, but it certainly complicates it. The difficult thing about alcohol is that we are all very unrealistic about how much we drink.

- 'I only had a couple of glasses' means you've probably had three or four.
- 'I don't drink very much' means you don't get drunk very often, but you still drink often and more than just a glass.
- 'I'm sober enough to drive' means you shouldn't!
- 'I'm a social drinker' means that you think drinking a lot is fine as long as someone else is doing it with you.
- 'Did you see how much so-and-so drank?' means you're in denial about the fact that you had almost as much.

- 'I never drink on weekdays' – except for the office lunch, that supper with friends, a drink with your sister . . .
- 'He insisted I have a drink' means you're blaming someone else.

This common denial about our intake of alcohol is not usually a problem. We have times when we rein ourselves in, others when we are a bit more indulgent, but our drinking can become dangerous to ourselves and others if we are under strain from external circumstances, and we are using alcohol in a vain attempt to cope with that strain. This is where depression comes in. If we begin to use alcohol inappropriately, then it can impact on depressive symptoms.

- A depressed person can begin to abuse alcohol or drugs in an attempt to relieve their low mood.
- Alcohol and drugs can make the symptoms of depression worse.
- Substance abuse can mean that the symptoms of depression are masked and therefore not treated.
- Drug and alcohol abuse are not compatible with the successful treatment of depression, and therefore recovery, because many antidepressant drugs interact badly with alcohol and recreational drugs, and also people drinking heavily will not take their medication reliably.
- Substance abuse raises the chances of suicide in a depressed person.
- Thirty-two per cent of people suffering from a mood disorder also show some form of substance abuse or dependency. We discuss ways to help control drinking in Chapter 6.

All these social factors linked to depression can only pose a threat to a person if for some reason they are already susceptible. Remember that different life events affect people in different ways, and any reaction should be respected. So you might feel a friend is making a bit of a meal of her old cat dying, but for the friend her animal's death seems emotionally overwhelming. Whether you understand or not, you will not help your friend by trivialising her problem.

PHYSICAL FACTORS

These are factors that have a physical component, and affect our general body health. The problem with some of these physical contributors is that the symptoms of depression can get mixed up with the symptoms of the illness, and so no help is forthcoming to treat the depression.

Chronic Pain

Depression is strongly associated with chronic pain, i.e. pain that is experienced over a long period. A high percentage of people suffering in this way will also experience major depression. There is no definite organic link between pain and depression, but the psychological impact of pain is huge, particularly because pain is invisible. No one else can experience your pain or appreciate the degree to which it affects you. If you break you arm or have a tumour, then others will understand more readily, but, for example, ongoing severe back pain can just seem like whingeing. If you are the victim of chronic pain, the accompanying disability and the lack of hope that the pain will ever be alleviated can wear you down and precipitate depressive illness.

Malfunction of the Endocrine System

The endocrine system includes the thyroid gland, and the adrenal and pituitary glands, which are responsible for the manufacture and dispersal of stress hormones such as cortisol. Cushing's syndrome – an endocrine disease – causes an increase in production of cortisol, which in turn reduces the efficiency of mood chemicals serotonin and noradrenaline. About half of all people suffering from this disease are also depressed. Studies have shown that raised cortisol levels are present in many severely depressed people, although it is not yet known whether high cortisol levels produce depression, or whether depression triggers high cortisol production.

Thyroid malfunction is also sometimes responsible for depressive symptoms. Anxiety and palpitations can be a result of high levels of the thyroid hormone thyroxine; lethargy and dejection can result from low levels of thyroxine.

Stroke

Some 30 to 40 per cent of stroke patients develop major clinical depression. There is still no evidence to explain why this should occur, although you might expect reactive depression to accompany such a disabling condition. Doctors researching in this arena believe that left frontal lobe damage to the brain can trigger the rapid onset of severe depression, whereas damage to the right side of the brain seems to trigger depression more slowly, with less severe symptoms.

Parkinson's Disease

In this disease, the levels of dopamine – a mood-enhancing neurotransmitter – are lowered in the brain. This not only affects the person's mobility and muscle function, but also promotes depressive illness. Recent research has shown that the area of the left frontal lobe in the brain associated with Parkinson's seems also to be linked to depression.

Seasonal Affective Disorder (SAD)

As we mentioned earlier, SAD sufferers experience depressive symptoms as a direct response to the reduced amount of light available during the dark winter months. This is thought to be as a result of the pineal gland producing too much melatonin, the hormone that helps us sleep.

Multiple Sclerosis

The myelin sheath – the fatty layer that protects the nerve paths in the brain and the spinal column – is damaged in this degenerative disease. But this does not explain why a large percentage of MS sufferers are prone to depression and mood swings, unless you take Professor Horrobin's model for depression into consideration and look at the levels of EFAs in a person with MS – research that has yet to be done.

Diet

A poor diet, devoid of vitamins, minerals and EFAs, can trigger depression. Low levels of B vitamins, vitamin C, folic acid, magnesium and potassium are particularly implicated in contributing to depressive symptoms. Equally, dietary habits that strip the body of nutrients, such as smoking, drinking alcohol in excess and eating foods rich in saturated fat, or to which you are intolerant – e.g. wheat, sugar and dairy products – are strongly linked to depression. We discuss this in more depth in Chapter 6.

Prescription Drugs

Medication given for other conditions can sometimes produce the symptoms of depression. Here are ten of the most common prescription drugs associated with depression, but, remember, they do not have this side effect in the majority of cases, so if you are taking any of the drugs listed below, there is only a small chance that the drug might trigger depressive symptoms. Consult your pharmacist when taking a new medication to check for possible side effects.

- Carbamazepine. Used as an anticonvulsant, antipsychotic and mood-stabilising drug.
- Chloral hydrate. Used as a sleeping drug.
- The oral contraceptive pill.
- Some beta-blocking drugs, such as hydralazine and clonidine. Used for lowering high blood pressure.
- Levodopa. Used for Parkinson's disease.
- Sulphonamide antibiotics. Used for bacterial infections.
- Benzodiazepines. Used to reduce anxiety.
- Corticosteroids. Used for rheumatoid arthritis, asthma and skin conditions.
- Pentazocine. Used as a painkiller.
- Amantadine. Used as an antiviral drug and also to treat Parkinson's disease.

Whenever symptoms of depression coincide with taking a new drug for another condition, or changing your levels of medication, your doctor should first consider whether the drug is implicated in your symptoms. Always tell your doctor what medication you are on, and whether you are taking it as prescribed.

Whatever the contributory trigger, or triggers, for your depressive illness, once you have identified them you can go a long way to avoiding them in the future. Just understanding the factors that make us vulnerable to this disease can also help eliminate the common view that depression is somehow our fault.

The EPA Theory

Now that we have looked at all the various contributory factors that experts have long held to be triggers for depression, it is time to look at the newest and most exciting theory about why we get depressed. The story is a good one, going back millions of years in time to when our brains began developing their human characteristics, and travelling forward to the point in the last century when Professor Horrobin began to realise that high levels of certain fats, essential fatty acids (EFAs, of which EPA is one), were fundamental to healthy brain function.

We look in detail at how EPA works on depression in the next chapter, but before we begin the tale of the fatty acid theory, here is a brief explanation of EPA's effect on the brain: EPA is an essential fatty acid which, when it enters the cells in the brain, helps to form a fatty layer that both protects the brain and enhances its ability to function at optimum speed and efficiency. We cannot easily make EPA in our body, we have to eat it in food and then convert it, but we all have a certain amount of this natural substance in our brain. The problem is that our modern diet and lifestyle have lowered the levels of EPA at which our brains function best, leaving us vulnerable to depression.

Dr Puri and his research colleagues are not saying that low levels of EPA always cause depression – there are perhaps millions of people out there with low EPA levels who are not depressives – but they are adding low levels of EPA as an important item, perhaps the key item, to the list of factors that, in a vulnerable person, might trigger a depressive episode. As a natural corollary to this theory, they suggest that replacing EPA therefore has a beneficial effect on the symptoms of depression. Dr Puri's research, and extensive studies carried out elsewhere, has now shown this to be true. The team also put forward the idea that raising EPA levels either through diet or supplementation, or both, might help to avoid a depressive episode in the future.

THE GENESIS OF THE IDEA

To appreciate fully the history of the EPA theory it is important to know something about our understanding of human evolution – the path that led us from ape to human. According to established scientific wisdom, our nearest relatives in the animal kingdom are the great apes: gorillas, chimpanzees and orangutans. We aren't descended from them as such, but modern techniques that can identify and decipher DNA (deoxyribonucleic acid) – our genetic code – show that we share a common ancestor. And in fact there are not a great number of genetic differences between us and chimpanzees, although those few differences have proved significant:

- We stand upright comfortably and consistently.
- We have a lot more body fat, even at birth, and our fat has a different distribution from that of apes, e.g. breasts and buttocks.
- We have a large, sophisticated brain characterised by creativity, imagination and speech.

- We have voluntary breathing control and a larynx developed for speech.

There is no evidence to show when some of these changes, such as increased body fat, decreased hair and changes in the structure of the larynx, came about, because they leave no obvious trace, but they are thought to have happened at least 3 million years ago. Brain size, what we ate and when we walked upright, however, are more easily charted through fossil bone analysis.

So if humans and apes are descended from the same original source, why are we not still like apes, or they like us? This is the sixty-four-thousand-dollar question, and over the last century there have been two markedly different propositions to explain this evolutionary conundrum.

The Savannah Dweller

The most widely held theory is that humans developed from the great apes when the apes came out of the forests and began to inhabit the African grassland, or savannah. But although apes are still predominantly vegetarian, there is evidence that the human diet changed significantly around 3 million years ago. Fossil remains tell us that our human ancestors had begun to eat a much more omnivorous (non-vegetarian) diet. Why did this come about?

The savannah theory goes like this. Humans evolved in response to the savannah environment. So, for instance, we began eating meat as a survival response, there being not enough vegetarian options in the dry grassland. And if we needed to eat meat, it is reasonable to assume we needed to develop hunting skills in order to catch the meat. Since hunting animals is not easy at the best of times, and requires a high degree of planning, co-operation, cunning and stalking skills, plus an ability to craft weapons, the body and brain evolved in recognition of this need.

So we became bipedal (standing on two legs), and our brains enlarged and developed the thinking patterns required to hunt successfully, which in turn distinguished us from our ape ancestors. There is, however, no explanation as to how this might have happened, why it happened, or why it didn't happen to the great apes as well and at the same time. The savannah theory is mainly supported by the many human fossils from that era – i.e. 3 million years ago – that have been found in savannah-like terrain.

The Aquatic Dweller

The second theory, and the one most germane to the EPA breakthrough, was first proposed by an Oxford University professor called Alister Hardy, and then taken up by journalist Elaine Morgan, who has written many books on the subject. Known as the aquatic ape theory, it suggests that humans went through a period when they were predominantly aquatic dwellers, i.e. they lived a large part of the time in the water.

The theory is based on the premise that when our human ancestors inhabited the savannah 3 million years ago we were already different from our ape relatives. The adaptations had apparently been brought about as a result of an aquatic phase, which happened around 7 million years ago when the African plain was flooded by the Red Sea. These adaptations included:

- We lost our body hair; fur is an impediment in water.
- We became bipedal; it is easier to fish, wade and swim as a bipedal, and if the plains were flooded we would need to keep our heads above water.
- Our body fat increased to keep up our body temperature in the water and aid buoyancy.
- Our breath control was developed as a result of fishing underwater.

When the flooded sea plain then became land-locked and eventually dried up millions of years later, the marine hominids then adapted again to the savannah, but by now they were on a different path – i.e. a human one – to their common ape ancestors. And this is why the fossil bones have been found in the savannah.

EFAS ARE PINPOINTED

David Horrobin first began to develop his own theory about human evolution in the 1970s, while he was working as Professor of Medical Physiology in a new medical school in Nairobi, Kenya. In the process of research into schizophrenia, he came to the conclusion that we evolved into humans rather than remaining as apes because of a relatively small change in the chemical make-up of the fat inside our brain. Professor Horrobin's theory differs from both the savannah dweller theory and the aquatic ape theory. He believes that at the time of our brain development, our ape ancestors were neither wholly savannah dwellers nor wholly aquatic dwellers, but semi-aquatic dwellers, i.e. we lived near lakes, rivers and marshes, 'thriving on the marginal interface between water and land'. Although the human fossil bones of this period were discovered in savannah, the remains were almost all centred on areas that had previously contained water, such as dried-up riverbeds, lakes and, later on, the seashore.

Horrobin's proposition is that our brain enlarged and developed as a result of the largely marine diet, rich in essential fatty acids (EFAs, of which EPA is one), which were available in abundance in these watery locations. He believes the serious savannah hunting came later, when the water had dried up and our brains had grown, making us mentally capable of getting our heads round the complexities of weapon-making and hunting.

A DIET RICH IN EFAS

The brain consists of mostly water, but the next most significant component is fat. The dry weight of the brain is made up of around 60 per cent fat, a fact that would surprise most people. And EFAs make up 20 per cent of that fat. The brain requires about 20 per cent of our energy intake to be maintained efficiently, although it accounts for only 2 per cent of our overall body weight. The brain controls the healthy functioning of both mind and body, so it makes sense that a well-nourished brain gives the best chance of a body firing on all cylinders, and a brain that is not depressed. To do this we need to eat a diet rich in nutrients that support brain function, particularly essential fatty acids.

Professor Horrobin believed this to be particularly true where mental health is concerned, proposing that a diet devoid of or low in EFAs might be a significant factor in mood disorders that target the mind, such as schizophrenia. His proposals, back in the late 1970s, were met with derision by the medical and scientific communities. However, since others have joined him in research to support his theory, and come up with some extraordinary results, the tide has finally begun to turn.

EFA LEVELS LINKED TO DEPRESSION

If it is true that there is a deficiency of certain essential fatty acids – such as EPA – in depressive illness, then a research study would expect to find a link between the intake of these dietary fatty acids and the occurrence of depression. In other words, the kind of diet we eat might be seen to influence whether or not we suffer from depression. One man's research graphically illustrates this crucial link. Dr Joseph R. Hibbeln,

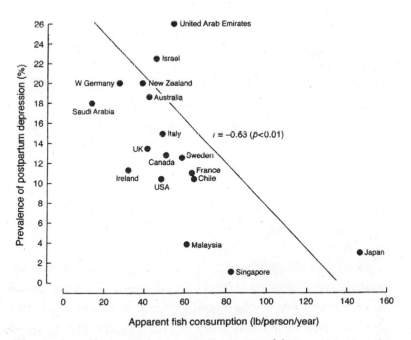

The prevalence of postnatal depression versus apparent fish consumption in various countries (after Hibbeln J.R., 1999).

a research doctor in the United States navy, whom Dr Puri frist met at a psychiatry conference in the late 1990s, carried out a study designed to discover whether there was a link between the intake of fish (oily fish contains high levels of EFAs) and the occurrence of depression in nineteen different countries, focusing particularly on postnatal depression (PND).

Looking at a wide range of studies published between 1993 and 1998 that detailed the incidence of PND in these countries, he related these findings to the levels of fish consumption (see diagram, previous page). As you can see, as the line denoting fish consumption goes up, the line denoting PND goes down. So countries such as Israel, Saudi Arabia, New Zealand and Australia eat less fish and have more postnatal depression, while countries such as Japan and Singapore, where fish forms a large part of the diet, have a low rate of depression.

Dr Hibbeln went on to do a number of other studies which built on his previous work. One particular follow-up study found that there was a marked relationship between suicide rates in men and seafood consumption. The higher the fish intake, the lower the rate of mortality from suicide, which is, of course, linked to depression.

Dr Puri was very interested in Dr Hibbeln's work. He began to look for other evidence that supported the theory of both Hibbeln and Horrobin that depression might be the consequence of a lack of vital fatty acids in the brain. To find this evidence he would, ideally, have wanted to examine brain cells of depressed and non-depressed people and check the relative levels of EFAs. But obviously you can't dig brain cells out of living people, so researchers did the next best thing: they examined their blood.

TESTING FOR EFAS

By examining a person's red blood cells we can get a pretty good idea of what is happening in their brain cells. This is because every cell in the body is the same in structure, and the EFAs are lodged in a double membrane, or skin, around the cell. Red blood cells, or erythrocytes, help carry oxygen in the blood to the various tissues and cells throughout the body – including the brain – and to study the red blood cell membrane for essential fatty acids requires nothing more traumatic than a normal blood sample from the depressed person for testing. For this reason, this has been a key method of checking for fatty acid levels in the nerve cells of a depressed brain.

In 1998 Rhian Edwards, David Horrobin, Malcolm Peet and others published the results of a study into the fatty acid levels of people suffering from depressive illness who were not at the time taking medication for their symptoms. What they found was that the red blood cell membranes of the depression sufferers had low levels of certain EFAs. By finding a low level of EFAs in their red blood cells, they concluded that there was, in all probability, also a lack of fatty acids in the nerve cells in their brain.

They then went on to do another study, this time also taking into account the other influences that affect fatty acid levels, predominantly the quantity of fatty acids being consumed in the diet, but also the factors that might reduce existing levels, such as social class, smoking and excessive alcohol consumption. They compared the blood from the depressed group of people with blood samples taken from a group of healthy people who were not depressed, but were the same age and had the same dietary and social habits as the depression sufferers. Again the study showed that levels of certain EFAs were lower in those who were depressed and also that there was a relationship between the intake of fatty acids and the degree to which the person was suffering depressive symptoms, i.e. the lower the intake the worse the depressive symptoms.

The exciting conclusion to both these depression studies, and to many others that were to follow, was that they pointed to a significant link between intake of fatty acids and depression – which had been Professor Horrobin's contention since the late 1970s.

OPPOSITION IN THE MEDICAL COMMUNITY

Yet despite the compelling evidence supporting these conclusions, when these researchers tried to share their findings with their peers they found the same problem that Horrobin had encountered for the previous thirty years: that most of the scientific community still refused to acknowledge Horrobin's fatty acid 'model' for depression as significant. You might wonder why no one seemed to take seriously a breakthrough that might be potentially life-changing for millions of people. It wasn't as if any of the scientists involved in the EFA discovery were anything but highly qualified and respected in their various fields of expertise.

The answer lies with the pharmaceutical industry in general. Drug companies are major funders of medical research, and it is simply not in their best interests to support research findings which may undermine the massive amount of money made from the sale of antidepressants worldwide. And the pharmaceutical factor affects research across the board, because it relates primarily to money. Academics are notoriously badly paid. Drug companies need them to do research, and also often pay them retainers to promote their product. As we mentioned earlier, most of the money relating to depression research in the last two decades has gone towards investigating the levels of brain chemicals such as serotonin, noradrenaline and dopamine in the brain, which the SSRI type of drugs address. So if the universities and academic community are seen to be promoting theories that might undermine this research, they are unlikely to get the funding from the drug companies upon which they depend.

Whatever the reason for this academic opposition, the fatty acid pioneers were undeterred, and gradually they began to see the fruits of their efforts. The research has moved on to identify not just EFAs in general as a factor in depression, but specifically the essential fatty acid EPA, and more and more doctors and scientists are now recognising the value of this breakthrough theory. This is how the EPA theory came into being, and radically changed the face of depression treatment. The other psychological, social and physical factors we outlined are still relevant contributors to making us vulnerable to depression, but the main biological trigger for depression can now be identified as low levels of EPA.

In Chapter 4 we explain exactly what EFAs and EPA are, where they come from, how the body metabolises them and how they are linked with depression through their interaction in the brain. We also chart Dr Puri's gathering of evidence to support the EPA theory, and find out more about the workings of the depressed brain.

Points to Remember

- No one cause of depression has been identified, just a number of contributory factors which when combined can trigger the disease. These factors are either psychological, biological, social or physical.
- Medical science is still not sure why one person suffers from mood disorders and another, in apparently the same circumstances, does not.
- Low levels of EPA have been shown to be a strong contributory factor in depressive illness.
- EPA supplementation has been proved to alleviate depressive symptoms.
- Depression is an illness, and although some of the contributory factors might seem to be elements in your life for which you can take responsibility, such as diet, reaction to life events and thought patterns, the fact is that none of us knows, until we have experienced depression, which elements in our life might trigger the disease.
- Think of depression as a cake, and the factors that contribute to it as the ingredients. There are many different methods, and many different ingredients, which can be used to make a cake.

Chapter Four

How Can EPA Help?

Mood disorders such as depression are centred in the brain, and most scientific research into this disease has focused on brain function. Therefore knowing how the brain works, in basic terms, will help you to understand the role EPA plays within the brain, and how it helps to support brain function as it fights depressive illness. So we are now going to take you on a brief scientific journey into the workings of the brain and the effect EPA has on it. And since EPA is a fatty acid, this will also include details about fatty acids, where they come from and what their significance is for a healthy brain. It is a fascinating story, and it explains a lot more about our mental and physical health than just the path to depressive illness.

How the Brain Works

The human brain is the most extraordinary organ in the body. It controls our immensely complex body function, acting as the ringmaster for all the other systems in the body, including both the unconscious mechanisms such as our heartbeat, breathing and digestion, and the conscious mechanisms such as speech and movement.

The story of brain function starts with the billions of nerve cells, or neurons, which create a mesh of electrical impulses throughout the brain. This mesh of electrical impulses acts like a huge circuit board, stimulating the various thought, motor and sensory pathways in the body, thus allowing us to do the simplest thing, such as scratch our head or whistle a tune, or the most complex, such as composing a symphony or discovering the theory of relativity – a range of sophisticated mechanisms that are not available to other mammals.

If there is a breakdown at any point in this complex electrical circuitry, then the activity in the brain is reduced. Research into depression, using brain imaging techniques such as Dr Puri used on Anthony's brain, shows that a depressed brain has a marked reduction in brain activity, implying that the electrical messaging system is malfunctioning in depressive illness. Here is a breakdown of the structures of the brain that make up the brain's circuit board and which are most crucial to the EPA story.

GREY MATTER

Imagine a surface the size of a tennis court. This is what the brain's cerebral cortex, or grey matter, would look like if it were laid out flat. Yet this enormous surface area, crammed with neurons and their little helpers, the glial cells, is crumpled up into folds so that it covers the other brain structures and fits neatly inside the human head.

NEURONS

Neurons are the nerve cells in the brain, around 100 billion in number. They have delicate tentacles protruding from the body of the cell, called dendrites and axons, which send or receive messages from other neurons in the brain in a complex electrical interaction for the purpose of stimulating activity in the numerous systems around the body. So, for example, you bump into a friend. Neurons will stimulate vision, recognition, the decision to speak, the words you choose, your hand reaching out to touch them, the sensation of that touch, the ability to process how your friend is reacting and your pleasure in the encounter. It is a chain reaction if you like, with the electrical impulses whizzing around your brain to achieve similar mental, physical and sensory sequences every minute of every day.

GLIAL CELLS

Glial cells, around 1000 billion in number, are responsible for supporting neurons by feeding them vital nutrients and providing the best biochemical environment for the nerve cells in the brain. So each of the 100 billion neurons are clustered about with hundreds of glial cells as back-up in their brain work.

NEUROTRANSMITTERS

Neurons are not actually connected to one another. So to help the electrical brain messages over the tiny gap, called a synapse, between one neuron and the next there are chemical molecules, called neurotransmitters, released from the neurons to bridge the gap. These include serotonin, noradrenaline and dopamine, and low levels of these particular culprits seem to be involved in depressive illness. This theory works on the principle that if there are not sufficient amounts of neuro-transmitter present, the electrical impulses within the brain, and therefore the rest of the body, will also be reduced, as the signals will not be getting from one neuron to the next so effectively, and both brain and body will cease to function properly, as happens in depression.

Parts of the Brain Implicated in Depression

There are many specific brain structures that are strongly associated with the symptoms of depressive illness, but it is important to remember that no one structure works alone. Our brain functions successfully by a sophisticated messaging system between all its separate areas. So you can see how if any one of these areas malfunctions, it can cause a trickle-down effect which then risks becoming a mood disorder. For example:

- The hypothalamus – an area of the brain – releases hormones which in turn trigger the pituitary gland to release more hormones, which in turn affect various glands in the body. These glands, including the thyroid and adrenal glands, then produce hormones which affect our mood, such as adrenaline (epinephrine), noradrenaline (norepinephrine) and cortisol. Depression is known to occur when, for instance, the levels of cortisol become too high. And the stress hormone adrenaline, if present at consistently high levels, can be a contributory factor in triggering depression.

- The pineal gland secretes the hormone melatonin, which helps us sleep. If this hormone is not being produced in the right amounts, then our body rhythms become disturbed, our sleep patterns go out of kilter, and depression can result. High levels of melatonin in the body are linked with seasonal affective disorder (SAD).
- The amygdala, a small walnut-shaped organ in the brain, plays a powerful role in emotional responses, such as fear and negative emotions. If this organ is damaged, then the person will not be able to respond adequately to normal emotional stimuli, which can make them anxious, which can then trigger stress hormones, which, as we said earlier, are implicated in depression.
- The frontal cortex in the brain, if over-stimulated, is assoc- iated with mania experienced by manic depressives. The different areas in the frontal cortex interact with each other via the neural pathways, and if one area is damaged and malfunctioning the others will also be affected, causing problems with memory, concentration, consciousness of self and emotional pain. Depression can be the result.

Brain imaging techniques have not only identified low levels of electrical activity in the brain of a depressed person, but also a reduction in the thickness of the cerebral cortex, or 'grey matter'. This is significant in the EPA story because when Dr Puri imaged Anthony's brain after he had been treated with EPA, he discovered to his amazement that Anthony's grey matter had begun to thicken and the nerve cells that are responsible for the electrical activity in the brain probably to regenerate. It was the proof Dr Puri needed that EPA worked as a treatment for depression.

This brief outline of the workings of the brain will help you understand how EPA is going to help your own brain fight depression. Now let's move on to the fatty acids that support this brain function.

EPA and Healthy Brain Function

What has EPA got to do with the healthy functioning of your brain? As we have already mentioned, EPA is an essential fatty acid. This essential fatty acid is known as omega-3. Both omega-3 and its fellow fatty acid omega-6 have been shown to be vital for overall brain health. So what is a fatty acid? A fatty acid is one of the 'building blocks' of a fat molecule. Glycerol, cholesterol and phosphorus are some of the other building blocks.

Essential fatty acids cannot be made in our bodies, we have to eat them in our diet. They are essential to us from the day we are born; newborn babies depend on their mother's milk for them, and later we must find them in other foods. So where do these fatty acids come from? There are two sources of fat in our body: some can be manufactured in the liver from proteins and carbohydrates; and the rest comes directly from the food we eat. The fat particles, after they have been metabolised, are transported to the brain via the blood. So the sequence of how fat reaches the brain goes something like this:

- Fats and oils eaten in the diet. Depending on the structure of the fatty acids, they are either saturated or unsaturated; the difference has a vital impact on our health.

Unsaturated fatty acids which are truly essential to our health are linoleic acid (omega-6) and alpha-linolenic acid (omega-3). EPA is a derivative of the latter. And these unsaturated fats are either 'poly' unsaturated (PUFA), or 'highly' unsaturated (HUFA), depending on the degree of chemical saturation. EPA is a HUFA, the most unsaturated fat.

- These fatty acids combine with other chemicals, or 'building blocks' such as glycerol, cholesterol and phosphorus, to become complex fat molecules known as 'complex lipids'.
- These lipids are carried in the blood to the cells in the brain, and other body cells.
- The brain then uses these fats to grow and create the complex interactions of all body systems.

How Do Fatty Acids Affect the Brain?

Complex lipids are made up of a number of different building blocks and fatty acids are one of them. The complex lipid that we are most concerned with when it comes to brain health is a phospholipid, which has the building block phosphorus as its essential component, and has a very important job to do. Most of the fatty acids in the brain are in the form of phospholipids, and these are responsible in part for the smooth messaging system between the neurons in the brain by ensuring that the electrical circuits are protected and insulated, like the plastic around an electrical wire, allowing the messages we want to get through to do so, and preventing the inappropriate ones, the crossed wires, from getting through. This is known as the 'phospholipid bilayer'.

If the phospholipids within the brain cells are made up predominantly of saturated fatty acids, because that is what we are eating in our diet, then since saturated carbon chains

tend to clump together and react slowly with other molecules, the brain cell membrane, and therefore the neuron
and neurotransmitter function, becomes sluggish and sticky,
and the electrical messaging system in the brain is slowed
down. However, when the phospholipids in the brain cells
are predominantly highly unsaturated fatty acids (HUFAs),
then the carbon chains are much more fluid, the brain cell
membrane, and therefore the neurons and neurotransmitter
receptors, can float freely in the cells, working at optimum
speed and efficiency, and as a result the brain messaging system
is much more successful.

Understanding HUFAs and Their Derivatives

There are two different kinds of HUFA: the omega-3 type
and the omega-6 type. Each type differs slightly in structure
and value, and to understand the EFA story we have to look
at how fats are broken down along chemical pathways in
the body to produce fatty acid derivatives such as EPA.

Imagine two different pathways, the omega-3 pathway,
and the omega-6 pathway. At the beginning of the
omega-3 pathway stands the 'parent' HUFA, alpha-
linolenic acid (ALA). At the beginning of the omega-6
pathway stands the 'parent' HUFA linoleic acid (LA). See
diagram, next page.

These two parent HUFAs, in themselves, are not implicated in brain health; their role is to act as precursors, or
parents if you like, to the fatty acid compounds, such as
EPA, which *are* essential to the brain cells. Further down
the omega-3 pathway, EPA is derived, and further still along
the pathway, docosahexaenoic acid (DHA) is derived.
Further down the omega-6 pathway, dihono-ganna

linolenic acid (DGLA) is derived, and further still along the pathway, arachidonic acid (AA) is derived. These HUFAs are then absorbed, via the bloodstream, into the phospholipid layer of the cell membrane in the brain.

Omega-3 Fatty Acids	Omega-6 Fatty Acids
ALA	LA
↓	↓
EPA	DGLA
↓	↓
DHA	AA

These are the four main HUFAs which are found in all healthy cell membranes. So this is what the essential fatty acid pathways look like:

Omega-3 pathway is:

- Alpha-linolenic acid (ALA): the parent compound. It is found in flaxseed, walnuts, soybeans, rapeseed.
- Eicosapentaenoic acid (EPA). It is found in oily fish, cod liver oil, eggs, and a small amount in chicken.
- Docosahexaenoic acid (DHA). It is found in oily fish, marine algae, liver and kidney.

Omega-6 pathway is:

- Linoleic acid (LA): the parent compound. It is found in sunflower, sesame, almonds, safflower and extra virgin olive oils.

- Dihomo-gamma linolenic acid (DGLA). It is found in evening primrose, starflower (borage) and blackcurrant seed oils.
- Arachidonic acid (AA). It is found in seafood, red meat and dairy products.

It should be true that if we eat enough ALA and LA, the parent EFAs, in our diet, we will be able to make sufficient quantities of the other four HUFAs. But this is not always the case in practice. A diet high in saturated fat can actually slow down the fatty acid pathways, so that the EPA, DHA, DGLA and AA are not incorporated in the phospholipids we mentioned earlier, and therefore brain development and function are impaired.

Why Choose EPA and Not Another HUFA?

Finding out which particular essential fatty acid in the omega-3 and omega-6 pathways was the most efficient in treating depression was one of the last parts of the jigsaw in this long run of research into the influence of fats on our mental health. So how did Dr Puri and his colleagues pinpoint EPA as the most successful HUFA with which to treat depression?

We have established that phospholipids – the complex fat molecules that are found in every cell in the body, and which protect and enhance the connectivity of the brain messages – are vital to a healthy brain and the avoidance of depressive illness. But why, if essential fatty acids in general are some of the essential building blocks that go towards the production of these phospholipids, choose EPA? Why not DHA or AA, or why not just give patients a supplement of LA, or ALA, the parent fatty acids which help spawn the derivatives such as EPA, DHA, DGLA and AA? Here are some of the reasons:

- EPA has been shown to prevent the breakdown of phospholipids by an enzyme called phospholipase, and so protects the brain messaging system. In other words, EPA helps maintain the integrity of the phospholipid bilayer.
- EPA can be derived from converted ALA, but, as we mentioned earlier, these EFA pathways can be slow and inefficient if sabotaged by a high intake of saturated fats and dietary pollutants, so the resulting amount of EPA in the brain might be too small to be helpful in treating depression if only ALA were to be given.
- Because Horrobin and his colleagues' research into the effect of EFAs on the brain began by looking at their effect on schizophrenia, Dr Puri's research led on from the schizophrenia research. At first Horrobin and his colleagues thought AA would be the HUFA most likely to have a therapeutic effect, but their trials with fish oils which attempted to single out the separate benefits of the various HUFAs then began to show that DHA, which is found in large amounts in a healthy brain, and in reduced amounts in the schizophrenic brain, might be the therapeutic winner. But when they did comparative trials with DHA and EPA on schizophrenic patients, they were astonished to find that the patients who improved substantially were the ones on EPA. Their improvement was consistent with the improvement you might expect with normal anti-schizophrenic drugs, but without any of the side effects.
- Dr Puri and his colleagues noticed that one of the associated symptoms of schizophrenia – depression – was also noticeably improved following the treatment with EPA.

- Dr Puri backed up the findings when he was successful with his first depressed patient tested with EPA, Anthony, and found that it worked well in treating serious depression as well as schizophrenia.
- This breakthrough was then further backed up by two major international studies (see box below), one Scottish, one Israeli, using EPA to treat depression, which came up with the same exciting result, and by Dr Puri's continuing success in his own practice.

So these various research strands led Dr Puri and his colleagues to choose EPA as the most successful of the essential fatty acids for treating even serious depression. They had finally discovered that EPA, rather than the other HUFAs in the omega-3 and omega-6 pathways, worked at least as well as, and in many cases much better than, standard antidepressant drugs, but without the side effects these powerful drugs might impose.

Breakthrough Research Studies

The Scottish Study

The first study, by Peet and Horrobin, was a randomised, double-blind, placebo-controlled trial carried out in Scotland, and involved seventy patients who were suffering from depression that was persisting despite ongoing treatment with standard antidepressant drugs. The trial lasted twelve weeks, and the background antidepressant drugs the patients were receiving were not altered during the trial. The results showed that the patients on EPA were better than the placebo group and showed significant improvement, after only four weeks, in all symptoms of depression.

The Israeli Study

The second study, also randomised, double-blind, placebo-controlled, by Dr Boris Nemets, Dr Ziva Stahl and Professor Robert Belmaker, was carried out in Israel with twenty depressed patients who again had not responded to conventional antidepressant drugs, and whose medication was not altered during the trial. The results were similar to the Scottish study, in that the patients in the group receiving the daily EPA and not the placebo showed significant improvements in their depressive symptoms after only three weeks, compared with the placebo group, who did not.

How EFAs Are Linked to Depression

You are all too familiar with how you feel when depression comes on. Your mood is low and your body and brain feel sluggish and exhausted, like a run-down car battery, just flickering with life, no more. And now you have read the science, you will understand that when you are feeling like this, the phospholipid layer in your brain cells has become thin and of poor quality because your EFA levels are low, and that your brain itself is running on empty, with none of the usual electrical messages criss-crossing the intricate circuit board.

So let's run through the process that turns a healthy, non-depressed brain into a sluggish, depressed one, and how EFAs are the cavalry riding up to rescue you from your depression. Here is a typical depression scenario:

- You are going through a difficult time in your life, your mother has just died and things are not going your way. You are eating food that is high in saturated fat. This means lots of croissants, biscuits, pastry, butter and cheese, and you are also drinking and smoking too much. Your mother had depression too.

- Your intake of EFAs is already low because of your diet, and those that you do eat are being beaten to the phospholipid layer by the lumpish saturated fats.
- The phospholipid layer in your brain cells is therefore sluggish and not at all mobile, and your grey matter begins to shrink.
- The neurons and neurotransmitters, serotonin, noradrenaline and dopamine, which pass the electrical signals around your grey matter, are now in trouble, because without the support of a healthy, fluid phospholipid layer they are in short supply and finding it difficult to keep up a lively messaging service. The messages keep going astray, are intermittent, or just take longer to pass round.
- You are beginning to feel less lively yourself, as the levels of serotonin, noradrenaline and dopamine fall, because these neurotransmitters really influence your mood. The more you have the better you feel, but these low levels are making you feel as if you've been switched off.
- You are now experiencing depression, with a low mood, no pleasure in life, a sense of despair and sleep disturbance.
- You seek help and begin taking the essential fatty acid EPA, and substitute the unhealthy saturated fats in your diet with healthier unsaturated EFAs.
- This healthy fat is carried in your bloodstream to your phospholipid layer and gradually, over a few weeks, replaces the saturated fat in your brain cells.
- Soon your phospholipid layer has a spring in its step, it becomes fluid and lively again. And your grey matter begins to regenerate, getting fatter and healthier.

How Can EPA Help?

- Your neurons and neurotransmitters breathe a sigh of relief. At last, the cavalry has come to save them. More neurotransmitters are released from the neurons and the messaging system is once more up and running, the electrical signals whizzing back and forth in the grey matter, galvanising all your body systems to get back to normal.
- Your depressive symptoms begin to disappear, your mood lightens and you start to feel hopeful about your future. You too breathe a sigh of relief. Your depression is over and your brain is once more healthy.
- You keep up a high level of EFAs in your diet, perhaps also supplementing with EPA, and your depression does not come back because the other contributory factors, such as feelings of low self-esteem or emotional trauma, although they will still affect you, will not so easily upset a strong, healthy brain and plunge it into a depressive episode.

Symptoms of Low Levels of EFAs

Obviously mood disorders are now seen to be a result of low levels of EFAs, but it is not just your brain that is affected when the phospholipid layer is not nurtured with essential fatty acids. Many other systems of the body are also disrupted. This is helpful in a way, because it can tell you in advance if you might be biologically vulnerable to a depressive episode, and that you need to increase your intake of EFAs.

Because these fatty acids are essential, we should all take a look at our diet and lifestyle and do all we can to promote high levels of HUFAs in our bodies. We discuss the ways you can do this in detail in Chapter 6, but here are some of the signs that your body might be low in EFAs. These problems will be as a result of prostaglandin imbalances, which are affected by a lack of EFAs. Prostaglandins are hormone-like body chemicals, made from the EFAs in the cell membrane, which regulate bodily functions in the heart, liver, lungs, brain, nerves and immune system, and are key to triggering the pain and inflammatory response. One prostaglandin in particular, called E1, is thought to be responsible for controlling several critical body functions. If your EFA levels are low, so too are your prostaglandins, and these low levels will hamper your fight against depression by lowering your general body health and resistance.

- You might suffer from dry hair, brittle nails and dry, itchy skin.
- You might be suffering from frequent infections. You get every cold, if you cut yourself your skin takes longer to heal, a cough settles on your chest.
- You have a low sex drive.
- You have urinary frequency and feel thirsty a lot.
- You might suffer from inflammatory illnesses, such as arthritis, eczema and psoriasis.
- You might suffer allergic reactions, such as hay fever or asthma.
- You might suffer from monthly cyclical breast pain and premenstrual syndrome.

If you are suffering from any of these problems, turn to Chapter 6 to find out how you can supplement your diet with EFA-rich food and supplements.

Habits that Strip the Body of Essential Fatty Acids

Along with enriching your intake of fatty acids, it is also worth taking a look at the ways your diet and lifestyle habits strip EFAs from the body, or hamper the conversion of EFAs into the phospholipid layer. (Check out some tips to remedy these habits in Chapter 6.) These habits do not necessarily cause depression – there are many people who eat an extremely unhealthy diet yet never succumb to depression – but they are a strong contributory factor in making the biological environment in your body ripe for a depressive episode if other factors are in place to trigger it.

Habits include:

- Eating high levels of saturated fat, i.e. too many animal products such as cheese, milk, cream, butter and fatty meat. These things are fine in moderation, but they should be balanced by large quantities of foods that contain omega-3.
- Eating high levels of trans-fatty acids (see box, next page). Again, we can't avoid these entirely unless we eat a very pure diet. The secret is to be aware of what you are eating. Check the labels.
- Eating high levels of sugar, i.e. cakes, sweets, chocolate, biscuits.
- A high alcohol consumption. Moderate drinking is fine, but often depressed people turn to alcohol as a panacea for their despair.
- Smoking cigarettes. These are never a good idea for anyone, but they are particularly unhelpful if you are trying to boost your EFA levels.
- A lack of certain nutrients, such as zinc, selenium and B6

in your diet. The body works synergistically with all the nutrient elements of the diet. Good vitamin levels greatly enhance the conversion of EFAs in the body.

- Constant dieting, which depletes nutrition levels.
- Eating too much processed food, because it often has high levels of the foods mentioned above. This is all right occasionally, but many of us eat a diet made up almost exclusively of processed food.
- Exposure to high levels of pollution. You can't help where you live, but if you boost your EFA levels your body will be much better able to cope with attack from pollutants.

What Are Trans-fatty Acids?

A certain type of food processing and refining, called hydrogenation, where healthy unsaturated vegetable oils are hardened to make saturated fats using high temperatures, is very common in the manufacture of spreads that mimic butter, commercial cakes, biscuits and other spreads. These fats are called 'trans fats' and are to be avoided if possible, as they actively reduce the nutrient value of essential fatty acids. With the high level of processed food now being consumed in the Western world, it is perhaps no surprise that diseases such as depression, which are now so strongly linked with low levels of EFAs, are on the increase.

Understanding the Effects of EPA on the Brain

Now we know why HUFAs are so important for brain health, let's look back at Anthony's story and see exactly what EPA does to the brain to stop it from being depressed. It wasn't enough for Dr Puri just to accept the discovery that EPA was a great treatment for depression, he wanted to know what was happening in Anthony's brain that made it so.

Dr Puri scanned Anthony's brain after his first consultation with him, when he had agreed to be a guinea-pig and try out EPA on his persistent depression. Then, following daily doses of EPA, Anthony came back for a second brain scan nine months later, and Dr Puri carried out other tests on his brain using a facet of the MRI technology (see box, next page) known as magnetic resonance spectroscopy, which enabled him to take a look at the fatty acid chemistry of Anthony's brain, i.e. what was happening to the EFAs inside his brain cells.

The results, as Dr Puri explained in Anthony's case study in Chapter 1, were absolutely extraordinary, and defied all expectations. Dr Puri, remember, would not have expected to see any changes in brain development in a fully grown adult, unless they were degenerative changes brought about by a disease such as Alzheimer's or dementia. Dr Puri's expectations were based on the fact that it was thought, until recently, that adult human brain tissue does not have regencrative qualities, and would not be expected to grow. The nerve cells and supporting glial cells – the ones responsible for stimulating all brain activity – in particular are not thought capable of reproducing once we become adults.

So Anthony's brain scan came as a complete surprise to Dr Puri: there was clear evidence of a thickening of the cerebral cortex, or grey matter, and reduction in the size of the brain ventricles, or chambers, indicating that parts of his brain tissue had actually grown and regenerated during the time he was taking EPA. Anthony's scan also showed a large increase in the amount of phospholipids in his brain-cell membranes, meaning that the EPA he had been taking was having a highly beneficial action on

Anthony's neurons and neurotransmitters, which, as we have already outlined, are so crucial in the electrical messaging of the brain.

Dr Puri discovered from Anthony's brain scans that EPA had actually enhanced his grey matter. And since the grey matter is the home of the neurons and neurotransmitters, if it is thin and unhealthy there will be fewer neurons and less mobile receptors for the mood-enhancing neurotransmitters, so the levels of serotonin will fall and you might suffer depression. However, if your grey matter is enriched and healthy, then there will be a greater abundance of healthy neurons and higher levels of neurotransmitters, and your depression will lift.

Recent American research studies carried out on rats have confirmed that brain cells do regenerate as a result of brain exercise, so we now know that adult mammalian brains are capable of brain growth, but in Anthony's case it is thought, although this is still not certain, that the EPA he was given acted by stimulating the stem cells – the cells from which our red and white blood cells are made – which form new brain tissue, or grey matter.

Magnetic Resonance Imaging (MRI)

Magnetic resonance is a phenomenon involving both magnetic fields and radio frequency waves. It produces clear, well-proportioned and easily understood images of soft tissues. In particular, MRI produces excellent, high-quality images of the brain. Not only can the ventricles of the brain be seen in detail, but even the cerebral cortex, or grey matter, is well defined, which is why MRI has become the imaging method of choice for the living human brain.

The scanning does not involve the use of X-rays or any other kind of ionising radiation, and is therefore generally safe, with one proviso. The technique uses a large magnet, so it is important that the person being scanned does not have any objects on or inside their body that may be magnetic, such as metal plates put in after bone fractures, hip replacements, heart pacemakers, metal sterilisation clips or IUD contraception devices. Careful checks are always carried out before using this scanning technique.

EPA and Other Brain Disorders

Dr Puri already knew EPA's potential for treating the brain disorder schizophrenia, but, faced with Anthony's brain scan results, he reckoned that if the nerve-cell membranes had been so enhanced by the treatment with EPA, then perhaps the same treatment would be effective on other brain disorders, such as Huntington's chorea, a progressive, inherited, degenerative disease of the brain. He decided to test out his theory. If this were true, then it would be an even more extraordinary break-through than he had previously imagined. EPA would have a huge potential not only for treating schizophrenia and depression, but also for dealing with debilitating brain conditions which had hitherto had no hope of a cure or even palliative treatment, conditions that cause much distress to their sufferers and those close to them, sometimes over an entire lifetime.

SCHIZOPHRENIA

He prescribed EPA to one of his patients who was suffering from schizophrenia (see Chapter 2, Contexts for Depression, p. 34). He had been suffering from this disease for many years and was taking no medication for his symptoms. Within a few weeks of being on daily EPA, almost all his symptoms went into remission, i.e. they disappeared at least for the present moment. Dr Puri also carried out image registration on the patient's brain, to discover that during the first six months of taking EPA his brain had begun to regenerate in the same way as Anthony's had.

It was also interesting to discover that this schizophrenic patient was experiencing other benefits. His ability to read and to spell had improved, his performance on a standardised reading test rising from below average before his treatment to above average levels afterwards, showing marked advances in reading speed, accuracy, fluency and comprehension. And this was after only three months. These positive side effects implied that his brain was beginning to function more efficiently as the EPA nurtured his grey matter.

HUNTINGTON'S DISEASE (HUNTINGTON'S CHOREA)

There is a one in two chance with every pregnancy that a parent with the Huntington's disease gene will pass it on to his or her children, who will go on to develop the condition in later life. The disease involves brain deterioration, finally resulting in dementia and death, and unfortunately at the moment there is no successful treatment for this devastating condition.

However, a professor at Monash University, Australia, Krishna Vaddadi, has long argued that fatty acids are of benefit in Huntington's disease, and, on the basis of his work, Dr Puri and others carried out a small trial on some patients in the severe end stages of the illness.

Of the seven patients, three received EPA daily, and four received a placebo. They scanned all seven patients before beginning treatment and after six months. Unfortunately, some of them moved their heads during the scanning procedure and therefore the brain scans of only four of the seven patients were capable of being analysed. Of the four scanned successfully after six months, the two on the placebo showed the expected increase in the size of their brain ventricles, i.e. their grey matter had decreased in size as is consistent with brain degenerative diseases. But the two who had been taking EPA showed the opposite. Their grey matter had increased in size and the brain ventricles were therefore smaller, just as Anthony's were. The two who had been taking EPA also showed a reduction in their unpleasant neurological symptoms.

A PREGNANT WOMAN'S BRAIN

It has long been held that pregnant women can sometimes be a bit dotty and not capable of being entirely reasonable – a contention hotly disputed by the women themselves – so Dr Puri was interested to see from the results of a study with which he was involved at Hammersmith Hospital, using consecutive MRI scans, that women's brain ventricles actually enlarge during the last three months of pregnancy, i.e. their grey matter shrinks! Professor Horrobin's explanation for this discovery was that the unborn baby is probably scavenging the mother's HUFAs to assist their own brain development. The good news is that postnatal brain scans on these women showed that their grey matter gradually grew back to pre-pregnancy proportions.

Dr Puri and his colleagues now have a substantial and ever-growing research base on EPA. And what all these studies show is that EPA has an extraordinary effect on the brain's ability to re-grow nerve cells and therefore improve brain function in all areas. The potential of EPA, therefore, is not just limited to treating depression – although that would be significant enough in the light of the millions affected by this debilitating disease – but extends to include a whole raft of brain disorders that have so far proved resistant to medical intervention. This is wonderful news for those suffering from diseases such as schizophrenia and Huntington's, where doctors faced with treating these illnesses have so far only been able to provide temporary relief from the symptoms, and then not always successfully. And, of course, wonderful news for anyone vulnerable to a depressive illness.

So that is the story of EPA. Now we move on to tell you how best you can incorporate this knowledge into your life, in order to help your current depression and to avoid getting depressed in the future.

In the next chapter we take a long look at the various different antidepressant medications you are probably taking right now for your depression, the side effects you might be experiencing, and the other more natural treatments you might have tried. We assess how these treatments stand, in the light of Dr Puri's breakthrough in depression treatment, and explain how you can enhance your current treatment options with supplements of EPA.

Most importantly, we answer the question you will all be asking: 'In the light of Dr Puri's research, do I still need to take antidepressants for my depressive illness?'

Points to Remember

- Depression and other mood disorders are characterised by reduced levels of electrical activity in the brain. The 'circuit board' is malfunctioning.
- This reduced activity is thought, in part, to be as a result of low levels of the brain chemicals serotonin, noradrenaline and dopamine, which prevent the neurons, or brain cells, from connecting properly.
- Dr Puri's theory is that these neurons and neurotransmitters do not function properly because they are not supported by a good supply of a specific fatty acid, EPA, which helps promote an efficient brain-messaging system.
- Omega-3 and omega-6 are the family names for types of essential fatty acids. EPA is an omega-3.
- Tests have shown on many occasions that EPA enhances the brain's capability to regenerate cells.
- Other brain disorders such as schizophrenia and Huntington's disease can also be helped by treatment with EPA.
- EPA is the supplement of choice in nurturing the brain so that it functions at optimum health and strength, and is less likely to promote depressive illness.

Chapter Five

Antidepressants versus Natural Treatments

The standard treatment for all types of depression – mild, moderate and severe – is antidepressant drugs. If you are currently experiencing a depressive episode therefore, and you have sought medical help for your symptoms, the chances are that you will now be taking this sort of medication. And because Dr Puri's breakthrough treatment is so new, even if you were to go to your doctor this week and be diagnosed with depression, you would probably still be offered an antidepressant drug. So what are these drugs, how do they work, and why would you be better off taking EPA? Because now, for the first time, you do have a choice. You can either go down the route of antidepressant medication, and risk having to deal with the possible side effects, or you can take natural EPA for your depression. In this chapter we answer these questions and outline what your real treatment options are in the light of Dr Puri's current research and clinical studies.

First, it is important to have as much knowledge as possible about how to approach your treatment. One of the problems with depression, as we have already explained, is getting the best treatment. We offer some hints on how to get the most from a consultation with your doctor when you go to them in a depressed state (because your GP is your first port of call when you are depressed), so that your treatment best suits your needs. We go on to explain how the antidepressants that most of you are currently being prescribed actually work, and why EPA is the safer and more reliable option for treating your depression, looking at the long-accepted theory behind antidepressant drug treatment, its history and why Dr Puri's research now challenges this theory. We tell you about how EPA can enhance your recovery from depression while you are taking your currently prescribed antidepressants, and help reduce the likelihood of your experiencing another depressive episode if you have suffered in the past. We then discuss in detail the various antidepressant medications currently on the market, and their potential side effects. These side effects will by no means affect everyone, but you should be able to recognise them in case you are one of the people who is affected.

We also examine the effectiveness of the other natural alternatives to antidepressants such as St John's Wort and Cognitive Analytic Therapy, which have both become popular in recent years, and we explain their place in your treatment options.

Armed with all this information, you will be better able to make proper choices about how you treat your depression.

This chapter is aimed at all of you whose lives are involved with depression, not merely those currently taking antidepressant drugs, including:

- Those of you who are currently taking antidepressant drugs for your depression.
- Those of you who are being gradually weaned off your antidepressants because your symptoms are less severe.
- Those of you whose antidepressant treatment is not working.
- Those of you are who are experiencing side effects from your medication which you cannot tolerate, or which are worrying and unpleasant.
- Those of you who are depressed but not taking anything for your depression yet and think you might need treatment for your symptoms.
- Those of you who have suffered from depression in the past and don't want to get it again.
- Those of you who are advising someone who is suffering a depressive episode.

Anyone who is in one of the categories listed above (apart from the last one) can benefit from taking a high-dose supplement of EPA to help relieve their depressive symptoms.

Visiting your Doctor

It is so important to seek help for your depressive symptoms. Even if you are not sure what is the matter with you, telling your doctor about your symptoms can only help your peace of mind. So don't sit it out by yourself, make an appointment with your GP and talk it through with them.

If you are depressed, when you do visit your GP you will not be at the peak of your ability to concentrate and take in information, nor be able to give a clear account of how you are really feeling, especially in the short time you have to talk to your doctor. You might feel embarrassed at being there at all, convinced that your symptoms are just the result of your own shortcomings, and all you will be focusing on is the hope that they will give you something to stop you feeling the way you do.

So you might well walk out of the surgery with an antidepressant prescription in your hand, get the drugs from the pharmacist and simply start taking them without much more thought about what you are taking or what these drugs might be doing to you. You might not even know for how long you are supposed to take the pills, or when you will know that they are not working. It is not easy to think of all these things in the brief consultation time allocated.

Now that you have a side-effect-free alternative in EPA, it is more important than ever to scrutinise the treatment your doctor is suggesting. You and your doctor should share the best information available. You must tell your doctor all the details of your depressive symptoms, so that it is easier for them to pinpoint depression, or any other condition. The doctor, on their part, must give you as much information as possible about your treatment options, the possible outcome, and any side effects you might experience from drugs you are prescribed. If your doctor is not yet informed about the benefits of EPA in treating depression, show them this book and explain that you would prefer a natural approach to your treatment.

Here are some tips to help this process:

- Write down all your symptoms at home, before you get to the doctor's surgery.
- If you know of a parent or close relative who has been depressed, mention it to the doctor.

- Tell your doctor if you are currently taking any other drugs, such as over-the-counter or recreational drugs.
- Tell your doctor if you have ever suffered from side effects when taking any drug.
- If your doctor prescribes a drug, find out what their experience is with this particular drug. Have they prescribed it successfully before? Are there side effects you should know about and how common are they? When you have heard the details about what they are suggesting, compare it with what you now know about EPA.
- If you are already taking medication, make sure you know how long you are expected to take the drug and how soon you should feel better. If the treatment doesn't seem to be working, go back to your doctor and consider taking EPA. (If you are taking antidepressants, and you feel they are working, you might be loath to rock the boat by changing your treatment, even if it is to this natural EPA. So it is good news that you can *supplement* your antidepressants with EPA to increase the speed of your recovery. They can be taken absolutely safely together.)
- Get the leaflet for your current medication, which should accompany all drugs and outlines optimum doses and side effects. Your pharmacist will have this, but might not always include it with your medication unless you ask. Check out your current prescription on the Internet or with your pharmacist. Being informed is vital when you are taking any medication. Never take anything you don't feel is relevant to your symptoms.
- If you are already taking an antidepressant and you experience any adverse side effects, consult your doctor at once; never change your drug dose without consultation.

- If you do not feel up to monitoring your own medication, ask someone else to help out.
- If you worry that you won't ask all the relevant questions, take someone with you to the doctor's appointment.
- If you feel that your doctor hasn't grasped the reality of the way you feel, for whatever reason, don't hesitate to make another appointment, this time taking a friend or family member to put your point more clearly.

Please remember never to stop taking your antidepressant drugs without proper medical supervision and access to this natural alternative.

Problems with Your Doctor's Choice of Antidepressants

When you go to your doctor with the symptoms of depression, how does the doctor decide which of the many available antidepressants they would be best prescribing? The truth is that the doctor has little idea of what will work for any particular person, as all the antidepressants are supposed to help depression. It is a matter of trial and error to see which seems to work best. In some forms of depression, such as bipolar disorder (manic depression), there is a more commonly prescribed drug that has been found to be the most successful. It is a combination of carbamazepine and lithium, which are antimanic and antidepressant. But getting the dose right is less straightforward, and monitoring the maintenance dose carefully can also be problematical. And if you are diagnosed with SAD you will probably be prescribed time in front of a light box. But for the majority of depression sufferers who do not have a particular context for their depressive symptoms, the doctor can pick any of the antidepressant drugs currently on the market.

Your doctor, for want of any other yardstick to use in prescribing antidepressants, will probably stick to the drugs with which they are most familiar, or they might make the decision based on market forces, prescribing an antidepressant that is new to the market or very popular, one that they have recently read about or that the drug companies have just delivered to the surgery. Or they might make the opposite decision if the practice cannot afford the more up-to-date drugs, and prescribe an older antidepressant simply because it is cheaper. Of course, this approach to finding the right antidepressant can be a hit or miss business. Sometimes the first drug works; sometimes several different drugs are tried before one begins to help. And there are some people for whom no antidepressant seems to help.

However, there is no doubt that in many cases antidepressants do work and the symptoms of depression are eased. We have been told there is a real breakthrough in antidepressant medication too, with the SSRI drugs such as Prozac and its newer cousins providing a highly effective cure for depressive illness. But the cost to the patient is often high. Every major antidepressant now available has a list of unpleasant side effects which range from mild to severe. This may sound alarming, but not everyone experiences unpleasant side effects while taking antidepressants, and some of you will be prepared to tolerate them for the time you are taking your medication. However, the fact that they exist is a real problem overall in depression treatment for a number of reasons:

- If you are severely depressed and taking medication that is working for your symptoms, but the side effects are intolerable, you will have to change your medication to one that might be less successful. Or you might be tempted simply to stop taking your medication, or not take it properly, because you dislike the side effects.

- If you are depressed and you know the only treatment is antidepressants with potentially unpleasant side effects, you may be frightened to seek help.
- Your doctor may be unwilling to explain possible side effects to you, in case you refuse a treatment that might be helpful, and then you (or those close to you) might not realise that your unpleasant reactions are the result of the drug, and not know to seek the appropriate help.
- It is bad enough being depressed without worrying about how the drugs you are taking might make you behave, as in some of the more disturbing side effects linked with SSRIs.
- Doctors on the NHS, often through no choice of their own, might prescribe the older generations of SSRIs such as Prozac, simply because the cost of these drugs has now fallen. The newer generations are said to have fewer side effects, but are more expensive.

Most doctors, however, are trying to relieve you of your depressive illness in the best way possible. But they are inevitably caught up in the problem that no antidepressant drugs are entirely predictable or side-effect-free.

Psychiatrists are more knowledgeable about the particular effects of certain antidepressants than GPs, and will therefore prescribe more specifically, but a person visiting a GP in a depressed state does not always have the inclination to wait to be referred to a psychiatrist – particularly on the NHS where waiting times can be long – and so will take the first drug the doctor offers. Later in this chapter we list the types of antidepressants and their side effects, so you will know what the potential problems are with any particular medication you might be prescribed.

Why EPA is the Safer, More Reliable Option over Antidepressants

There are three other reasons, apart from the potential side effects of antidepressant medication, why we believe you would be wiser to choose EPA rather than antidepressant drugs for your depression, even though antidepressants often work well in reducing existing depressive symptoms.

- Antidepressants do alleviate depression, but they do nothing to prevent a further depressive episode.
- The long-held theory of the biochemistry of depression, known as the monoamine theory, does not satisfactorily explain the origins of depression, nor why antidepressant drugs actually work. Dr Puri's fatty acid theory for the biochemical origins of depression offers answers on both counts with regard to EPA, backed by solid scientific research and trials, which is why he and his colleagues now challenge the validity of the monoamine theory.
- Because of the validity of Dr Puri's scientific theory, EPA is much more reliable than antidepressants in relieving depression. He has not had a failure in treating depression with EPA, whereas the same cannot be said for antidepressants, even though they are often successful in alleviating symptoms.

TACKLING THE RECURRENCE OF DEPRESSION WITH EPA

Let's look first at the fact that although antidepressants may be successful in relieving your current bout of depression, these drugs in no way address the very real possibility that once you have succumbed to depression, there is a chance that you may succumb to further episodes in the future.

Studies do not clearly answer the question of how many depressive episodes a person who is vulnerable to this illness can expect over a lifetime, because many of the statistics only relate to the severely, hospitalised depressed, and many people with mild or moderate depression, as we have already discussed, do not seek treatment for their symptoms. But a general medical assessment puts the average number at between three to six episodes over a lifetime. Manic depression sufferers tend to have a more frequent recurrence, and women with mild depression tend to relapse more often, although no one knows why this should be, in either case. These statistics do not take into account the duration or severity of an attack, nor the period of time a person might have between bouts, but even given that the figures are only averages, they still pinpoint the fact that depression is a recurring illness. Therefore any drug designed to treat this condition should also address the problem of recurrence, but because of the side effects and the powerful nature of antidepressants it is not considered wise to use them prophylactically to prevent future bouts of the illness. So although antidepressants deal with your current symptoms, after your depression has lifted you will live with the knowledge that your depression has a good chance of coming back at some later stage. Talk to anyone who has recovered from depression and you will find that this is a common fear.

However, this need no longer be the case. EPA has been shown in Dr Puri's clinical research not only to relieve depression, but also to keep it at bay when the EPA supplement, which is safe to take long term, is taken on a daily basis. EPA achieves this by continuing support to the phospholipid layer in the brain. Patients of Dr Puri who have had their depression alleviated with EPA and stayed on a daily EPA supplement have not suffered further depressive episodes. However, previously depressed patients who have not kept up their daily EPA supplement once their symptoms have disappeared have, in some cases, found their depression returning. So EPA successfully tackles an important element of depression, which antidepressants don't begin to address, and it does it naturally.

THE EPA THEORY VERSUS THE MONOAMINE THEORY

Moving on to the second reason why we believe you would be wiser to choose EPA over antidepressants, let's take a look at Dr Puri's reason for considering that the monoamine theory has a flawed logic. To understand this, we have to go back to the beginning of antidepressant drug treatment and examine this theory, which is behind accepted medical opinion as the cause of biochemical depression, and which has been used as the basis for why antidepressants work.

The monoamine theory about the biochemistry and treatment of depression has been taught in medical schools for the last fifty years without challenge, until Professor Horrobin, Dr Puri et al. began seriously to question it in light of their research into fatty acids and the brain.

Chance Discovery of the First Antidepressants

How did the drugs which have been used since the 1950s to treat depression come to be used as antidepressants? The popularity of antidepressant medication is at an all-time high, as the number of people suffering from depression increases every year. Twenty million prescriptions for these drugs were dispensed in Britain in 2001, a rise of 700 per cent in just ten years, and the figures for other countries in the Western world are similarly alarming. Because of this popularity, new antidepressants appear on the market regularly, as pharmaceutical companies battle for the lion's share of one of the most profitable businesses on the planet. Yet although new drugs are constantly coming on the market, they are designed to have basically the same action on the depressed brain as the ones back in the fifties, with the same theory behind them. So how did it all begin?

Accepted medical belief is that antidepressants act on the neurotransmitters in the brain to alleviate the symptoms of depression. They do this in different ways, depending on whether they are the old-style antidepressants or the new SSRIs. So you might think, perhaps, that the first antidepressants were developed because research had shown what was happening to the brain during depression – i.e. that the neurotransmitter chemistry was imbalanced – and that doctors had then searched for, and found, the drug that would change this. What actually happened was the other way round. In the 1950s two synthetic chemicals were accidentally discovered to have antidepressant properties, and then doctors developed the theory of what happens to the brain during a depressive episode to explain the action of these drugs. In other words, the drugs came first and the theory of depression came second.

Back in 1951 British doctors treating patients for tuberculosis (TB) noticed that when two particular drugs were used the patients' mood lifted. At virtually the same time, French doctors noticed the identical effect and their findings were announced at a conference in 1952. These findings caused great interest and excitement in the medical world. These two drugs were found to be monoamine oxidase inhibitors, known as MAOIs. Monoamines are a specific type of neurotransmitter molecule responsible for producing noradrenaline, dopamine and to some extent serotonin. Low levels of these brain chemicals, as we have already mentioned, are present in depressive illness. The enzyme monoamine oxidase is an enzyme that normally breaks down neurotransmitters. If this enzyme is being inhibited from breaking down the neurotransmitters, then it follows that there will be higher levels of noradrenaline and serotonin in the brain, and therefore enhanced brain activity and less depression.

Another happy scientific coincidence occurred around 1952 which was to produce a further antidepressant drug. While testing a new drug on schizophrenics, Swiss chemists discovered that, although the drug was no good for treating schizophrenia, it was successful as an antidepressant. These drugs were called tricyclics. Tricyclics, like MAOIs, worked by acting on the levels of neurotransmitters in the brain. They blocked the re-uptake of monoamine neurotransmitters, specifically noradrenaline, i.e. they prevented the neurotransmitters being sucked back up into the receptor cells in the neuron, thus increasing the levels of noradrenaline and to a lesser extent serotonin available for brain connectivity. So they had a similar effect to that of MAOIs, but by a different route.

The Monoamine Theory

Back in the 1950s, it was thought that medical science had cracked the problem of depression, and the monoamine theory of depression was born. This theory held that the level of monoamine neurotransmitters – mainly noradrenaline – in the brain was fundamentally linked to depression and that the biochemical cause of clinical depression was low levels of these neurotransmitters in the brain.

Then research moved on, and soon it was discovered that low levels of noradrenaline alone were not responsible for depressive illness, and the scientists turned their attention to the other main neurotransmitter in the brain that is associated with depression, serotonin. The monoamine theory was given another focus. Scientists were now saying that depression was caused by low levels of either noradrenaline or serotonin, or both, in the brain.

Drugs that raised serotonin levels soon began to take over from the predominantly noradrenaline-focused tricyclic and MAOI drugs, and pharmaceutical companies came up with Selective Serotonin Re-uptake Inhibitors (SSRIs), such as the much vaunted fluoxetine, or Prozac. SSRIs work by blocking the reabsorption of the neurotransmitter serotonin from where it is needed in the gaps between the brain cells or neurons. So, just as the tricyclics do with noradrenaline, SSRIs prevent serotonin from being sucked back up into the neurons, the result being higher levels of serotonin, increased brain connectivity and less depression. Since the 1950s, therefore, all classes of antidepressants synthesised in the laboratories of pharmaceutical companies worldwide – including the new-generation SSRIs – have been designed in accordance with the monoamine theory, their aim being to increase monoamine neurotransmitters in the brain.

Problems with the Monoamine Theory

If the monoamine theory has delivered a type of drug that mostly relieves the symptoms of depression, then the fact that some researchers find it flawed should not matter to the average depression sufferer. But if they are right, and the monoamine theory is *not* sound, and therefore the accepted main biochemical cause of depression is not low levels of neurotransmitters, but instead low levels of essential fatty acids – which has now been shown to be the case – then it not only explains why EPA works so consistently well in curing depression, and keeping depression at bay, but also gives all depression sufferers a good reason to choose EPA over antidepressant medication. Because by doing so they are choosing a strong scientific theory for their depression treatment, which has been proven time and again in depression studies and research, and which addresses the very heart of their brain-cell membrane to stop depression at source, instead of a poorly understood drug treatment that happens to alleviate, in the short term, the symptoms of a particular depressive episode for reasons that still, after nearly half a century, are not fully understood by the scientific community.

What were the factors, then, that made some researchers question the monoamine theory and its status as the main biochemical cause of depression?

1. The delay in the time the antidepressant takes to act

If the monoamine theory is correct, and depression is caused by depletion of neurotransmitters in the gaps between the neurons, then reversing this depletion in the way the different classes of antidepressants do should lead to an immediate reversal of the symptoms of depression, because it is known that the action of these drugs increases the levels of neurotransmitters in the brain within hours.

However, there is generally a baffling delay of a fortnight between taking an antidepressant and the symptoms of depression beginning to be alleviated. Why are the increased levels not relieving the depression sooner? The fact is that no one knows, and this delay is not explained by the traditional monoamine theory, despite it being the mainstay of the modern psychiatric understanding of depression for so long. You might imagine that perhaps all drugs that act on the brain's neurotransmitters take a similarly long time to act, but this is not so. Anyone taking a sleeping pill knows that they don't have to wait a fortnight before getting a good night's sleep.

2. The action of reserpine

Reserpine is a drug that acts as a tranquilliser, and it is the generally accepted medical view (based on the monoamine theory) that this tranquilliser also causes depression because it causes a depletion of monoamine neurotransmitters in the gaps, or synapses, between the neurons in the brain.

However, a drug trial done at the Maudsley Hospital in London in the 1950s found that in fact reserpine, far from causing depression, actually acted as an *anti*depressant. This trial has been overlooked by the monoamine theorists for many years, and major textbooks on psychiatry still ignore this trial and maintain that reserpine is a depressant, probably partly because the pharmaceutical industry became so set on the lucrative antidepressant path, which was based firmly on the monoamine theory. But it made Dr Puri and his colleagues realise that there was more to the biochemistry of depression than just neurotransmitter depletion. He and his team went on to develop the fatty acid model for depression (see page 75), which provides a consistent scientific explanation for why the brain becomes biochemically depressed. Most of us, surely, would prefer to know that any treatment we are offered has a strong scientific reason for its use to relieve our depression.

THE RELIABILITY OF EPA OVER ANTIDEPRESSANTS

The final reason why we believe you should choose EPA rests on reliability. The antidepressant approach to treating depression is less reliable than EPA, because EPA tackles the root biochemical cause of depression, whereas antidepressants merely tackle one of the consequences of the biochemical cause of depression. Dr Puri has shown that the depressed brain is one where there are low levels of EFAs in the brain-cell membrane, known as the phospholipid layer. These low levels mean that the brain cells are less mobile, and as a consequence fewer neurotransmitters are released, the grey matter shrinks and brain activity slows down, causing the symptoms of depression. Antidepressants merely restore levels of neurotransmitters – one of the consequences of a starved phospholipid layer – to relieve depression. So treating depression with antidepressants is a bit like treating a boil with antiseptic cream and a sticking plaster. The boil will probably go away eventually, but a more successful, reliable, long-term way of treating boils would be to boost the person's immune system to fight infection and get to the bottom of why the person might be vulnerable to boils in the first place. EPA works in this way to restore brain activity at the very heart of the brain cell to relieve depression, and therefore works more reliably than antidepressant drugs in lifting depression. Dr Puri has been able to treat even the most severe cases of depression, such as Anthony (who, remember, had been failed by antidepressant treatment), successfully with EPA.

Antidepressant Drugs and their Side Effects

We have now detailed how antidepressant drugs work, and why it would be more sensible to treat your depression with EPA rather than antidepressants, but since many of you will currently be taking antidepressants, it is important for you to understand as much as possible about the drugs with which you are being treated. In this section we look at individual antidepressant drugs in more detail. On the next page is a table which presents each family of antidepressants, starting with the newer, most commonly prescribed drugs called SSRIs, as these are the ones you are most likely to come across, then moving on to the older, now less frequently prescribed tricyclics and MAOIs. The table charts briefly what type of drug each is, how they work on depression and any potential side effects. This table is not supposed to be a comprehensive guide, as that would be a book in itself, so we have only mentioned the most common drugs in each family in use at the present time. This is a guide for anyone taking these drugs, to allow you to check the potential side effects and help you make an informed choice about your ongoing treatment and possible supplementation with EPA. Remember, many people will not experience side effects when taking antidepressants, so don't be alarmed by some of the potential problems with these drugs. They are only 'potential'.

SSRIs (Selective Serotonin Re-uptake Inhibitors)

This new generation of antidepressant drugs are now the drug of choice for treating depression because they have fewer side effects than the older anti-depressants. It could be said that they are now over-prescrbed, doctors some-times giving these drugs to their patients as a cure for stress or unhappiness as well as depression.

The Most Commonly Used SSRIs

- *Fluoxetine*: trade name Prozac.
- *Paroxetine*: trade names Seroxat (UK), Paxil (US).
- *Sertraline*: trade names Lustral (UK), Zoloft (US).
- *Citalopram*: trade names Cipramil (UK), Celexa (US).
- *Fluvoxamine*: trade names Faverin (UK), Luvox (US).

How These Work

These drugs increase the levels of the neurotransmitter serotonin in the brain by preventing the existing serotonin from being reabsorbed into the cells.

Common Side Effects

These include: sexual dysfunction, such as delay or inability in reaching orgasm, loss of libido, loss of appetite and weight loss (although increased appetite and weight gain have been reported when taking citalopram), allergic reactions, dry mouth, nervousness and anxiety, headache, insomnia, tremor, dizziness, hallu-cinations, drowsiness, convulsions, the appearance of breast milk, sweating, movement disorders and bruising.

In addition to acting on receptors for the neurotransmitter serotonin in the brain, SSRIs also act on serotonin receptors in the gut. This leads to side effects in the digestive system such as: nausea, vomiting, dyspepsia, abdom-inal pain, diarrhoea and/or constipation.

Caution!

People have described the effects of taking SSRIs as feeling 'better than well', but using a drug to cope with your daily reality is a dangerous path to go down if you are not actually suffering from depression. It is wise never to take a drug that you don't actually need.

However, SSRIs are very successful drugs in the treatment of depressive symptoms, with fewer complaints about the common side effects that plagued the older antidepressants. They have also been found to be relatively safe in overdose. But there is one proviso to the enthusiasm that has greeted these SSRI drugs. There have been reports suggesting a possible link between usage of these types of drugs and suicidal and violent tendencies, although a causal relationship has not been established.

SNRI (Selective Noradrenaline and Serotonin Re-uptake Inhibitor)

This drug is prescribed as an alternative to an SSRI, although it has a similar action.

- Venlafaxine, trade names Efexor (UK), Effexor (US).

How This Works

SNRIs work in the same way as SSRIs, but they act to raise levels of noradrenaline as well as serotonin.

Common Side Effects

These include: dry mouth, nausea, headache, drowsiness, dizziness, nervousness, constipation, increased sweating, insomnia, painful joints, painful muscles, visual disturbances, a drop in blood pressure on standing, passing urine more frequently and tinnitus (ringing in the ear).

Caution!

Occasionally convulsions may occur as a result of treatment with venlafaxine. If this happens the drug should be discontinued.

NARI (Selective Noradrenaline Re-uptake Inhibitor)

This drug is also used as an alternative to SSRIs and SNRIs.
* *Reboxetine*: trade name Edronax (UK). Not available in US.

How This Works

It raises the levels of the neurotransmitter noradrenaline in the brain by blocking the reabsorption of existing noradrenaline.

Common Side Effects

These include: dry mouth, constipation, increased sweating, dizziness, insomnia, a drop in blood pressure on standing, vertigo, pins and needles, a rise in the resting heart rate, impotence and urinary retention (mainly men).

NaSSA (Noradrenergic and Specific Serotonergic Antidepressant)

This is one of the newer antidepressants recently introduced on to the market.
* *Mirtazapine*: trade names Zispin (UK), Remeron (US).

How This Works

Mirtazapine is thought to act by improving the transmission of noradrenaline and serotonin between the neurons.

Common Side Effects

These include: increased appetite, weight gain and jaundice.

Caution!

If jaundice occurs the antidepressant should be stopped and medical advice sought.

Nefazodone

This is another new antidepressant drug.
* *Nefazodone*: trade names Dutonin (UK), Serzone (US).

How This Works

It selectively blocks the re-uptake of noradrenaline to increase levels of nor-adrenaline in the brain.

Common Side Effects

These may include: dry mouth, sleepiness and sedation, nausea, dizziness, visual problems, weakness, light-headedness, confusion, a drop In blood pressure on standing, chills, fever, constipation, pins and needles.

Trazodone

This drug is not related to other currently prescribed antidepressants, either in terms of its molecular structure or pharmacologically.
* *Trazodone*: trade names Molipaxin (UK), Desyrel, Trialodine (US).

How This Works

It increases the availability of serotonin.

Common Side Effects

These may include: dizziness, drowsiness and light-headedness. And some-times anxiousness, blurred vision, constipation, dry mouth, headache, poor concentration, muscular pain, nausea, nervousness, shortness of breath and vomiting.

Caution!

Sometimes it causes a skin rash, or in men, priapism – inappropriate and/or painful erection of the penis. In either case, a person should immediately stop taking the trazodone and seek urgent medical help.

Tricyclic Antidepressants

These drugs are less often used in treating depression these days because of their raft of unpleasant side effects and the fact that an overdose can prove fatal.

- *Amitriptyline:* trade names Triptafen (UK), Elavil and Endep (US).
- *Clomipramine:* trade name Anafranil.
- *Imipramine:* trade names Tofranil and Janimine.
- *Nortriptyline:* trade names Allegron (UK), Aventyl and Pamelor (US).
- *Amoxapine:* trade names Asendis (UK), Asendin (US).
- *Doxepin:* trade names Sinequan (UK), Adapin, Sinequan, Zonalon (US).
- *Trimipramine:* trade name Surmontil.
- *Lofepramine:* trade name Gamanil (UK).

How These Work

They raise levels of noradrenaline and serotonin in the brain by inhibiting the reabsorption of neurotransmitters noradrenaline and serotonin.

Common Side Effects

These may include: dry mouth, blurred vision, constipation, urinary retention (difficulty in passing urine), nausea and sedation.

Caution!

The last side effect could be potentially dangerous if you are driving or operating machinery. Tricyclics also affect the heart and circulation, causing changes in heart rhythm, and even a relatively small overdose can lead to problems with the heart, convulsions, respiratory failure, coma and death. This makes the drug difficult to prescribe in quantity without constant monitoring of the patient to check they are taking them correctly.

Tetracyclic antidepressants

These act in the same way as tricyclic antidepressants.

- *Mianserin* (non-proprietary).
- *Maprotiline*: trade name Ludiomil (UK and US).

How These Work

They raise the levels of serotonin and noradrenaline in the brain.

Common Side Effects

These are similar to those of the tricyclic antidepressants. However, the tetra-cyclic drugs are less likely than the tricyclics to cause these side effects. Rashes are common with maprotiline treatment and at higher doses there is a risk of convulsions. Treatment with mianserin can lead to a reduction in white blood cells, so that the person taking this drug is more prone to infections. Those taking mianserin will therefore have regular blood tests to check the levels of white blood cells, and treatment should stop if an infection is present. Other side effects of mianserin include jaundice, arthritis and painful joints.

MAOIs (Monoamine Oxidase Inhibitors)

These are the oldest antidepressant drugs, and are not used very often these days because of their unpleasant side effects.

- *Phenelzine*: trade name Nardil.
- *Isocarboxazid*: trade name Marplan.
- *Tranylcypromine*: trade name Parnate.

How These Work

These drugs block the activity of the enzyme responsible for breaking down neurotransmitters noradrenaline and serotonin.

Common Side Effects

These include: dry mouth, blurred vision, constipation, urinary retention, seda-tion, nausea. Also liver damage, agitation, tremor, sweating, headache, insomnia, convulsions, rashes, bruising, sexual disturbances, an increased appetite for food, weight gain and abnormalities in heart rhythm.

Many other medicines react badly with MAOIs, such as some over-the-counter cough mixtures and nasal decongestants, and also most other classes of anti-depressants, including tricyclics, SSRIs, NARIs, SNRIs and NaSSAs (see below).

Caution!

If certain foodstuffs are eaten or drunk when a patient is taking an MAOI, then a potentially life-threatening reaction can occur. These are foods containing a substance called tyramine, such as: cheese, yeast extracts – Marmite, Bovril and Oxo – and fermented soybean extract, alcohol, pickled herring, seasoned game, offal, avocado, broad beans and caviar. If these foods are eaten with MAOIs, the interaction can cause a dangerous rise in blood pressure.

There have been some cases of death occurring when patients have taken an MAOI with one of the antidepressants listed above. Dangerous interactions between these antidepressants and MAOIs can sometimes occur if a person is changing from one antidepressant to another because his symptoms are not responding. It takes time for an antidepressant to clear from the body, and at least two weeks should elapse between taking an MAOI and any of the above antidepressants, and also two weeks before eating any of the inter-active foodstuffs mentioned.

If a person is changing *from* another antidepressant *to* an MAOI, for instance changing from an SSRI, such as Prozac, it can take up to five weeks before the active ingredient in the SSRI is washed out of the body.

Because of these dangers, a person taking any MAOI antidepressant should ask their doctor for a treatment card to carry with them at all times, which lists the precautions they should take in respect of food and drink and other medicines that need to be avoided. Other side effects include: MAOIs can also have addictive qualities because of an action similar to that of amphetamine ('speed').

Withdrawal

SSRI Withdrawal Syndrome

This withdrawal syndrome – which follows the too-sudden cessation of treatment with SSRIs – occurs with all the currently available SSRIs and usually begins within a week of stopping SSRI treatment. It can be very unpleasant, and is characterised by a variety of physical and psychological symptoms, although it normally resolves within three weeks. It is important therefore to reduce the dose of your SSRI gradually under medical supervision. The common effects of too-sudden withdrawal include: dizziness, nausea, vomiting, lethargy and fatigue, headache, instability in walking and insomnia. Also sometimes vertigo or feeling faint, pins and needles, anxiety, diarrhoea, irritability, tremor and visual disturbances.

Non-SSRI Antidepressant Withdrawal

If one of these types of antidepressants – namely tricyclics or MAOIs – has been taken regularly for eight weeks or more, stopping the drug suddenly may cause the following side effects: nausea and vomiting, loss of appetite, headache, giddiness, chills and insomnia. Sometimes a person's mood may become clinically 'high' – mania or hypomania – and necessitate hospital treatment. In the case of MAOIs in particular, a person may experience restlessness, anxiety and panic if the drugs are stopped too suddenly. It may take around four weeks of gradual dose reduction to avoid these withdrawal reactions, and longer if the person has been taking antidepressants for a year or more.

Don't Suddenly Stop Taking Your Antidepressants

We have mentioned this before, but it is extremely important that when treatment with a particular antidepressant is being stopped, the drug be withdrawn gradually – except in cases of medical emergency, for example if convulsions occur as a result of taking venlafaxine. This is because, after taking an antidepressant regularly, stopping it suddenly may lead to withdrawal symptoms. These symptoms differ between the SSRIs and the other antidepressants as highlighted above. However, while you are gradually reducing your antidepressant medication you can be taking an EPA supplement safely at the same time, which will do the job your antidepressant has been doing except without any side effects.

Think Twice before Starting Antidepressants

Until recently, if you were depressed and desperate to feel better, you had few choices. You would be advised to begin a course of antidepressants. This course may be successful, but in many cases it is not. And even if it is, antidepressants will only deal with your current depression, they will not protect you from experiencing another bout of depressive illness in the future. You might experience unpleasant side effects too. Or you could soldier on and hope your depression will go away by itself, which, of course, it usually does in the end. This is what as many as two-thirds of depression sufferers have done in the past, either because they were unable to admit they needed help, or because they were frightened of taking antidepressants. But although the depression might go away eventually, the problems suffered in the interim can be extreme. Depression, as we have discussed, has a high cost and can affect our relationships at home and at work, it can affect work itself, and in its severest form it can leave us vulnerable to taking our own life.

Whether or not you are one of the people who experience unpleasant reactions while taking antidepressants, or during their withdrawal, the list of possible side effects from all anti-depressants makes sobering reading. And although these drugs have been shown to be effective in treating depression, as we've seen, there are a number of reasons why you might think twice before embarking on a course of this type of medication:

- You might be prescribed the drug that the doctor's prac-tice can afford, or the one the drug company is promoting, rather than the one best suited to your needs.
- Your doctor may not know which antidepressant is most suitable, as they are all supposed to treat depression.
- You might suffer from any number of unpleasant side effects.
- Your antidepressant may not work and you may have to try another one. This would mean your symptoms could take a long time to disappear.
- Antidepressants don't stop you from experiencing another bout of depression at a later date.

Other Natural Treatments for Depression

As you can see from the information above, there are many health risks associated with antidepressant treatment. And because of all the problems relating to these powerful drugs, the search has been on for many years to find a natural alternative to them. The researchers have turned to herbal remedies, looking back at the plant substances that have been used in the past in relation to mood disorders, and to psychological therapies that address the emotional problems thought to be a substantial trigger in depressive illness.

As a result there are now a number of other natural treatments for depression which have become increasingly popular in recent years, particularly for mild and moderate depressive symptoms where people are reluctant to risk a course of heavyweight antidepressants. The two most popular are the herbal remedy St John's Wort – which is one of Germany's leading antidepressant drugs and accounts for a large percentage of the market there – and the 'talking' therapy, cognitive analytical therapy (CAT). So in the light of Dr Puri's breakthrough with EPA, is there still a place for these other natural treatments for depression?

ST JOHN'S WORT

St John's Wort has had more media coverage than any other treatment for depression except Prozac, but, despite its high profile, and more research than many of the herbal remedies have enjoyed, there is as yet no conclusive study that shows it to have antidepressant qualities effective enough to tackle major depression. *Hypericum perforatum* is thought to be called St John's Wort because its bright yellow flowers appear around 20 June, the saint's day. The plant is native to warm, moderate climates, such as Europe and the United States, and was originally used as an antibacterial in wound healing. The active ingredient is hyperforin, and although no one quite knows how it works, it is thought to act on depression by raising the neurotransmitters noradrenaline, serotonin and dopamine in the brain. It is also said to have sedative properties and be helpful in calming anxiety and excitability.

How Effective is It?

An evaluation in the late 1990s of a number of studies into St
John's Wort's antidepressant qualities seemed to show that it
was more effective than a placebo in treating mild or moderate
depression and the symptoms of SAD. But many scientists were
not happy with the way these trials had been conducted, and
in 2001 a large American study done under more rigorous
conditions concluded that the herb was no more effective in
relieving depressive symptoms than a placebo. More trials are
under way, but it must be acknowledged that, despite negative
findings, many millions of people seem to have been helped
by this remedy over the years in dealing with their depression.

What Are the Side Effects?

Because St John's Wort is a herbal remedy, many therefore
assume that it is automatically safe to take. And, taken alone
and in the recommended doses, St John's Wort does seem to
be safe. The worry about side effects is focused on the herb's
reaction with other medication. Studies have shown that it
should not be taken in conjunction with other depression drugs,
particularly MAOIs and SSRIs, as it might cause an allergic
reaction in some people. Also the HIV anti-viral drug indinavir, the immuno-suppressant cyclosporin, the anti-coagulant
drug warfarin, the heart drug digoxin and the contraceptive
pill may have reduced effectiveness if taken with St John's Wort.
This is because the herb has been shown to increase the activity
of a particular group of liver enzymes which are involved in
metabolising these drugs. Self-medication with St John's Wort
is safe if you take the above contraindications into account,
but it is important to check with your doctor that you are
really suffering from depression before commencing treatment.

This is to eliminate the other illnesses that might mimic depression.

How Does It Compare with EPA?

To judge by the confusing, contradictory results of many of the studies into St John's Wort, and the fact that other medications, particularly antidepressant medications, can interact badly with the herb, EPA is a more reliable natural treatment if you are suffering from depression. Also, this herbal remedy is not successful for severe depression. Not only are there no adverse side effects with EPA, but also the scientific studies are both rigorous and conclusive about its benefits. EPA is a substance that, as we have already said, nurtures our brains at a fundamental level to prevent and cure depression, whereas St John's Wort treats existing symptoms and has a much less reliable success rate.

COGNITIVE ANALYTICAL THERAPY (CAT)

This therapy has been shown to be particularly successful in treating depression. We mentioned the pioneers of the cognitive approach, developed by Aaron Beck and Albert Ellis into Cognitive Behavioural Therapy (CBT) in the 1970s, back in Chapter 3. In the last decade behavioural therapy has become increasingly popular as an alternative to long-term psychoanalysis, perhaps because many of us find the concept of addressing our current behaviour and reactions easier and less frightening to deal with than delving into the hidden traumas of our childhood, as psychoanalysis does. But there is now a therapy, CAT, which combines examination of past traumas from childhood and behavioural techniques for dealing with the symptoms it throws up.

CAT is goal-directed: the first sessions identify unacknowledged influences from your childhood which might be contributing to your present unhappiness, such as unresolved loss or neglect; subsequent sessions offer techniques for changing your day-to-day responses and thought patterns which have stemmed from these unhelpful influences. The sessions are structured and usually number sixteen in all, so you will not be put off by the prospect of open-ended analysis that might last for years.

How Effective is It?

CAT does not work as fast as an effective antidepressant medication or EPA in alleviating depressive symptoms, but it has been shown to be highly successful, particularly in reducing the occurrence of future depressive episodes. This is because it addresses the way you think and why you think this way, helping you understand the distorted light in which you view the world. It is not always easy to recognise your negative thought patterns, because you have probably been unconsciously thinking this way all your life. For instance, you might automatically jump to negative conclusions. Even a common, everyday incident, such as a boyfriend not phoning when he said he might, will make you leap to the conclusion that it is because he doesn't love you, that he doesn't love you because you are unlovable, that no one will ever love you for this reason, and that he is definitely in love with someone else who is prettier and cleverer than you. When he does phone and apologise, you overreact and accuse him of all sorts of neglect and betrayal for which you have absolutely no evidence. He then decides you are too much like hard work, and the relationship founders, confirming all your paranoia.

CAT promotes personal awareness and gradually increases confidence and self-esteem, so reducing the likelihood of you falling into depressive illness in the future.

Make sure you find a therapist you trust. If you are not happy with a therapist then you will not be able to take full advantage of the sessions. It can initially be frightening to expose your inner thoughts to a stranger, but most people find the experience of unburdening their fears to someone who is trained to understand both comforting and a tremendous relief.

EPA alongside CAT

The therapy works well in conjunction with antidepressants, but would work even better while taking an EPA supplement. Supporting your biochemical pathways at the same time as rebuilding your emotional strength is an effective two-pronged attack for those with the type of destructive behavioural responses that can contribute to depression.

EPA: The Treatment of Choice

Dr Puri's revolutionary breakthrough in treating depression means that now you can be confident in obtaining a safe, side-effect-free treatment for your problem which is even more likely to alleviate your symptoms than antidepressant drugs. You no longer have to risk antidepressant medication and its potential side effects and failure rate to treat your depression, nor a less successful natural alternative such as St John's wort. You can choose a treatment based on solid scientific research that goes to the very heart of the biochemical cause of depression and successfully tackles your problem at source. Look at the many advantages of taking EPA, the natural supplement, over antidepressant drugs:

- EPA is a naturally occurring substance.
- EPA has side effects, but they are all good, including healthier skin, hair and nails, protection against heart disease, chronic fatigue syndrome, skin conditions, 'economy class syndrome' and many other conditions (see Chapter 7). There are no unpleasant side effects with EPA. The only people who should not take EPA or any fish oil supplement are those already on anticoagulant medication (see box below).
- EPA is a more reliable treatment for mild, moderate and severe depression than antidepressants.
- EPA works on depressive symptoms as quickly as anti-depressant drugs, often more quickly.
- EPA, if taken regularly, reduces the likelihood of your depression recurring.
- You will be more likely to seek help for your depression if you feel there is a natural treatment that will success-fully alleviate your symptoms.
- EPA can be taken alongside your current antidepressant medication to speed your recovery.

Caution! People taking anticoagulants such as warfarin or heparin, which thin the blood to avoid blood clots, should not take EPA or other fish oil supplements without medical advice, as otherwise their blood-clotting time might be too prolonged.

So there you have it. EPA really has been shown to be a revolutionary breakthrough in the treatment of depression. Yes, other treatments, such as antidepressants and St John's Wort, can also be successful in alleviating symptoms, but given the success rate of EPA, coupled with the lack of side effects and EPA's ability to prevent recurrence of the condition, this natural treatment is a clear winner when considering your best course of action when you realise you are suffering from depressive symptoms.

In the next chapter we move on to explain how you can obtain EPA as a depression treatment and how you can modify your diet and lifestyle to include lots of brain-nurturing essential fatty acids to make you healthy and resistant to future bouts of depression.

Points to Remember

- EPA has a strong scientific basis for its success in treating depression, whereas antidepressant treatment has not.
- All antidepressants have side effects, including the new SSRIs. These can range from relatively minor ones such as nausea, dry mouth and dizziness, to more distressing ones such as loss of sexual function, to potentially life-threatening ones such as convulsions and heart disturbances.
- Prescribing the right antidepressant can be a hit-and-miss affair, unfortunately often led by market forces rather than by medical knowledge.
- It is always important to understand as much as possible about any medication you are taking and to seek advice if you are worried or having problems.
- EPA can be taken safely in conjunction with antidepressant medication. Do not take it with anticoagulant medication however (see box, previous page).
- EPA is a much more reliable natural alternative for treating depression than St John's Wort because, unlike the herbal remedy, it has no side effects and has strong scientific studies to back it up.

- Cognitive Analytic Therapy is a good psychological treatment for depression, and can be supplemented with EPA for maximum benefit.

Chapter Six

Treating Depression with EPA

The first part of this chapter deals with treating your depression with the EPA supplement Dr Puri advises. We want to give you the confidence to use this supplement instead of antidepressants, but currently most doctors still prescribe the usual drugs, so we outline a strategy for taking charge of your own treatment using natural EPA. This information applies to those of you who are not yet taking anything for your depression, those of you who would like to come off your antidepressant medication and take EPA instead (remember not to come off your drugs without seeking medical advice), those of you who would like to enhance your antidepressant treatment with EPA, and those of you who are not currently depressed, but have been in the past and would like to avoid another depressive episode.

The second part of this chapter looks at how diet and lifestyle changes can enhance your general health and your overall levels of EFAs to help protect you from future bouts of depressive illness. Let's begin with Dr Puri's suggestions about how to supplement with EPA to relieve your depression.

Supplementing with EPA

There are two ways we can consume EPA. One is in the food we eat, and the other is in supplement form. Diet alone, however, is not sufficient to treat the symptoms of a depressive episode, because the levels of EPA are not found in a high enough concentration in a normal diet, so if you are depressed you will need to take a larger dose of EPA in supplement form.

There are several high EPA supplements currently available in Britain, the United States and Europe. These include eye q, VegEPA, Morepa, and Maxepa. At the time of writing, eye q is sold in the UK in Boots, Superdrug, Tesco and Morrison's supermarket. You can also obtain it, and the other supplements, on the Internet by going to the manufacturer's website (see resource section). The other supplements mentioned are expected to be available from chemists, health-food shops and other supplement outlets by spring 2004 at the latest.

VegEPA is the newest high EPA supplement, and is particularly interesting as it is completely vegetarian. This may seem surprising at first, since we have said that EPA is derived from fish oil. But in fact the fish manufacture their EPA from plant cells in the first place. VegEPA is similarly derived from plants, using a process that emulates the way in which fish create EPA. The capsules of VegEPA are also vegetarian, rather than being made from gelatine, as is the case with most other supplement capsules. A vegetarian alternative to fish oil EPA is also important for those of you who are allergic to fish products, or worried about the possible high toxicity levels in fish (see Oily Fish, p. 163).

Unfortunately, as this is such a new treatment, a high EPA supplement is not currently available on the NHS. This means that you will have to fund your own treatment until such time as it is included as a prescription option.

HOW TO TREAT YOUR DEPRESSION WITH A HIGH EPA SUPPLEMENT

Before you decide to treat yourself by using a high EPA supplement, it is advisable to get a diagnosis for your depression, in case your symptoms indicate another medical condition. But if you have experienced depression before and recognise the symptoms all too well, it is not necessary to get another diagnosis from your doctor. If you do see your doctor, they will probably not be familiar with EPA. So if they diagnose you with depression they will probably suggest you follow the standard route and take antidepressants. But you don't need to do so any more. If your depression is in the mild category (see Chapter 2), meaning that you are not severely depressed and considering suicide, you can buy your own supply of one of the high EPA supplements mentioned above, and take it as Dr Puri advises instead of resorting to antidepressant drugs.

However, this course of action raises some questions about how your doctor will respond and what sort of help and support you can expect from them. The answer is that support for treatment with EPA will vary depending on your particular GP. But there is a growing understanding that EPA is successful in treating depression – you need only take a quick look at the Internet – and the more enlightened doctors will be happy to support a treatment that has been shown to be so successful and to have such a strong scientific research base and clinical trials behind it. Other doctors, on the other hand, may be less enthusiastic and will try and persuade you to stick to antidepressants. Here are some tips for getting support for your treatment choice from your doctor:

- Take this book with you to your consultation and show your doctor the evidence for EPA.
- Explain why you don't want to take antidepressants: you are worried about the side effects, you prefer a natural product, you want the best chance of getting well and you don't want your depressive symptoms to return.
- Suggest your doctor takes a few minutes to look up EPA on the Internet.
- Explain that you would like their support in taking this breakthrough treatment option.
- Remind your doctor of all the thousands of depressed people who come through their surgery every year, and how wonderful it would be to be able to treat them with a natural, side-effect-free product.

If your doctor still refuses to support you in your choice of treatment, Dr Puri suggests you go it alone and treat yourself with a high EPA supplement, as the treatment plan is simple to understand and easy to implement. Flying in the face of medical advice may worry you, but if you remember that millions of people endure the symptoms of depression without any medical intervention at all, it seems less alarming. If you feel that your depression has a psychological trigger (see Chapter 3) as well as the biochemical, low EFA factor, then as well as taking an EPA supplement for your depression, it might help to see a cognitive analytic therapist (see Chapter 5), who will help you to come to terms with the psychological problems, such as low self-esteem, that might have triggered your present bout of depression. The best way to find such a therapist is either through your GP or through word of mouth.

One time when medical intervention is vital is if you are experiencing serious suicidal thoughts and your life is in danger. If this is the case and you are suffering from severe depression and have suicidal tendencies, you should get immediate medical attention as a matter of urgency. Your GP is the first port of call, and they will probably refer you to a psychiatrist if you are actively thinking of suicide. In cases of severe depression the highly purified ethyl-EPA is the best supplement to take. However, this can only be prescribed by certain doctors as, at the time of writing, it is not licensed in the UK, so is only available on a 'named patient' basis, meaning that it has to be specifically recommended by a specialist such as Dr Puri. At the moment there are only a handful of doctors who will prescribe ethyl-EPA for severe depression, but that number is undoubtedly set to increase when the substance becomes licensed in the future. In the meantime, show your doctor this book and ask him or her to find a specialist who will prescribe the purified EPA supplement for your severe depression. If this is not possible, take antidepressant drugs alongside an EPA supplement, so that your drug treatment will be enhanced.

EPA Dosage

Once you have decided to take a high EPA supplement for your depression, how much should you take and what can you expect from this supplement treatment?

For mild to moderate depression
Take 1000 mg of EPA a day. Check the details on the packet of the high EPA supplement you choose to determine how

many capsules you need to take to make up this amount each day. This is a completely safe dose for everyone, except those taking anticoagulants for heart disease (see below). Remember that if you are vegetarian or allergic to fish you should opt for VegEPA. This dose of 1000 mg a day is the optimum beneficial amount for treating your depressive symptoms. Dr Puri's research shows that your symptoms of mild or moderate depression will not be improved any faster by taking a higher dose. You should see an improvement in your symptoms within four weeks, and your depression should have disappeared completely within three months.

If, in the unlikely event that you do not see any improvement in your depression symptoms within three months, and you have been taking a high EPA supplement regularly at 1000 mg a day for that time, then see your doctor, as your symptoms may be the result of another medical condition. But remember, a high EPA supplement is a very effective general health supplement, and you can only benefit by taking it.

Caution! For those taking anticoagulants, you must consult your heart specialist about your anticoagulant therapy before taking an EPA supplement, because high EPA supplementation, as well as being effective as an antidepressant, is also an effective anticoagulant. If you take a high EPA supplement along side anticoagulant drugs you risk thinning your blood too much. It is possible to replace your current medication with a high EPA supplement, but this must never be done without medical advice (see Chapter 7 for the benefits to the heart of EPA).

To avoid further depressive episodes

If you have suffered depressive episodes in the past and are obviously prone to depression, but you want to avoid a recurrence, Dr Puri advises taking a maintenance dose of a high

EPA supplement for the rest of your life. This would mean taking 500 mg a day. This dose will support your brain function and prevent you suffering further depression.

As we have mentioned before, EPA has no unpleasant or worrying side effects, so you can take a high EPA supplement with confidence that all it will do is make you feel well again. It makes sense for all of us prone to depression to take a daily maintenance dose of EPA, but if you choose not to do this and your depression does recur, you can immediately go back on the 1000 mg a day recommended for alleviating those symptoms.

RAISING YOUR EFA LEVELS WITH DIET AND LIFESTYLE

EPA, like the other omega-3 and omega-6 fatty acids, does not occur naturally in our body, so we have to eat foodstuffs or supplements which contain these EFAs in order to maintain a high level in our brains. Apart from taking an EPA supplement, the other way to improve your levels of EPA, and EFAs generally, is through your diet and lifestyle options. Although, as we have said, diet alone is not sufficient to treat depression – for instance a can of sardines is only roughly equivalent to two capsules of eye q – a diet high in EPA and EFAs is important in order to support the phospholipid layer in the brain and so help avoid depressive episodes. Also, a high EFA diet is beneficial for general health.

If you are depressed you might not feel like paying attention to what you eat until your symptoms have improved with EPA, but even small modifications can help raise your essential fatty acid levels, and the rest of this chapter is devoted to explaining the various dietary and supplementary sources of EFAs, and how we can modify certain lifestyle habits, such as eating too much saturated fat, smoking and stress, to enhance the metabolism of these fatty acids in our system.

Essential fatty acids are vital to overall body health, not just brain function. They are necessary for the production of prostaglandins, the body chemicals that regulate bodily functions in the heart, liver, lungs, brain, nerves and immune system; they provide energy, maintain body temperature, insulate nerves and cushion and protect body tissues. The World Health Organisation (WHO) now suggests that EFAs should make up at least 3 per cent of our total calorific intake. A deficiency in EFAs is now associated with diseases such as cancer, heart disease, asthma, skin conditions such as eczema, attention deficit hyperactivity disorder (ADHD) and arthritis, as well as schizophrenia and depression. And we have already detailed the stunning effect of EPA on the brain.

Keeping healthy is a good defence against all disease, including depression. If our body systems are firing on all cylinders, we will not only be less vulnerable to attack from illness, but we will also be able to fight off the symptoms more readily. So it makes sense to eat a generally healthy diet, exercise and reduce our stress levels. And particularly for healthy brain function, we should also make sure that we eat a diet that is rich in fatty acids such as EPA. So to put ourselves in the best position to avoid suffering from depressive symptoms, we must pay attention to what we eat, know what we should avoid eating, and adopt healthier lifestyle habits, all of which will enhance our levels of EFAs and so nurture the phospholipid layer so vital to brain health.

The Problem with the Modern Diet

The modern diet has become woefully lacking in essential fatty acids. The biggest problem is processed food. Before the advent of modern food preserving and processing, we ate a more natural diet which was seasonal and mostly fresh. But for many of us today our diet consists almost entirely of food that has been tampered with to enhance its shelf life or make it more convenient for us to prepare and eat. This means high levels of saturated and trans fats, which if they are present are incorporated in the cell membrane and the phospholipid bilayer instead of HUFAs (see Chapter 4), and make the cell membrane rigid and the brain messaging system faulty, contributing to depressive illness. It also means we neglect fresh food, such as fish, green vegetables, nuts and mono- and polyunsaturated oils. Even the oils we do buy are often extracted and refined with processes such as hydrogenation, which makes the vegetable oils more stable but which destroys the essential fatty acids and therefore their health-giving properties.

A typical daily menu for a modern adult in Britain might consist of:
Breakfast: white toast, butter, tea or coffee.
Elevenses: biscuits and coffee.
Lunch: sandwich made of white baguette, margarine, tuna mayonnaise, fizzy drink, bag of crisps.
Tea: chocolate bar, tea.
Supper: ready-cooked, processed supermarket pasta dish, half a bottle of wine, a satsuma.

This menu is virtually EFA-free, and it is full of saturated fat and drinks such as tea, coffee and alcohol, and it is made even worse if cigarettes are included. Eating such a diet prevents existing essential fatty acids from being converted into the fat layer in the cell membranes of the brain. Even the tuna in the sandwich is tinned, so although it is an oily fish and potentially a good source of omega-3 fatty acids, the canning process might have destroyed some of the fatty acid goodness.

Yet the person eating this sort of diet might be in blissful ignorance of their problem, because this eating pattern has become so standard. The government health agencies have made some serious healthy nutrition drives in recent years to educate the public into eating more fresh fruit and vegetables, vegetable oils and oily fish, a campaign which the supermarkets have taken up, but it is still the case that most adults in Britain today eat an average of no more than one or two portions of fruit and vegetables a day, if that, and probably even fewer of the dark green vegetables, such as spring greens, Brussels sprouts and broccoli, or the vital oils that are such an excellent source of EFAs. This poor diet will only enhance the likelihood of a person vulnerable to depression experiencing a depressive episode, and will do nothing to help alleviate any existing symptoms of depression.

Not All Fats Are Bad

Many people, when they do address their diet and begin to eat more healthily, lump all fats together as health villains that will make them overweight, with the result that they cut down on the fats that are actually good for them, the EFAs. The Western world has become almost allergic to the concept of fat in the last two decades. Every other product you see in the supermarket today is 'low fat', from ready meals to dairy products, spreads, crisps and biscuits. This is because obesity has now become a serious problem, burgeoning in the same way as depression in the last decade. Although there is not thought to be any link between obesity and depression, diet plays a strong contributory factor in both conditions.

But it is not the healthy fats that are causing the problem. It is the saturated fats, including low-fat products, which are most often hydrogenated, saturated or trans fats, and we are not doing ourselves any favours in the battle with our weight by eating them instead of the nutritious oils which are full of essential fatty acids, such as olive, walnut, rape and sesame.

What are the unhealthy fats?

Saturated fat, as we mentioned earlier, makes the cell membranes in our brain and body tissue less mobile, and therefore reduces efficiency in all our body systems, making depression more likely and also increasing the risk of heart disease. Saturated fat mostly comes from animal sources. You can recognise it because it is generally hard at room temperature, like butter, cheese, lard. But full-cream milk and cream also have a high saturated fat content, and so do some oils such as coconut and palm oil.

Trans fat, which is fat that has been refined and hydrogenated, or hardened, turns healthy unsaturated vegetable oils into unhealthy saturated fat and should be avoided as much as possible in your diet. It can actually lead to a deficiency in essential fatty acids by tying up the metabolic processes like a broken key in a lock and preventing EFAs from progressing along the metabolic pathway from the parent omega-3 and omega-6 and being converted into the vital EPA, GLA, DHA and AA. Experts believe these trans fats are one of the biggest causes of EFA deficiency and the resultant health problems it causes. They are found in many commercially made cakes, biscuits, crisps, processed meat and ready meals. There is no law to insist that manufacturers of processed food list the trans fat content yet, but if you avoid processed food wherever possible, you will also avoid the damaging trans fat.

And the healthy fats?

These are the unsaturated fats which should make up the largest proportion of fat in your diet. They are either monoun-saturated or polyunsaturated, depending on the number of hydrogen atoms attached to their carbon-atom backbone. Most vegetable oils are a combination of the two, but predominantly one type.

- Monounsaturated fats include olive, almond, peanut, hazelnut, avocado and rapeseed.
- Polyunsaturated fats include sunflower, walnut, soya bean, pumpkin, corn and sesame. All essential fatty acids are polyunsaturated fats, but not all polyunsaturates are EFAs. These are the healthiest fats to eat, but unfortunately the polyunsaturated oils we buy in the supermarket are not always what they seem.

Pure, unsaturated, unrefined oils are health-giving, and are more easily metabolised than their saturated fat counterparts, not to mention their benefits to brain function. Taken in moderation, good quality oil is beneficial and will help in your fight against depression. When buying oil, try to buy cold-pressed, extra virgin oils, as these are less refined and have retained the most nutrients.

Poor Nutrition and Depression

It is not uncommon for someone who is depressed to find that their eating patterns go haywire. There is no one partic-ular eating pattern associated with depression, although a severely depressed person will tend not to eat much at all and will subsequently lose a lot of weight. Those with mild or moderate symptoms might go off their food too, or they might eat more, or they might binge eat – i.e. eat a lot at once, then nothing – or they might just eat the wrong things because they can't be bothered to cook or shop as they normally would.

Food and drink are strongly associated with mood. We eat to celebrate or as part of socialising, but we also eat to comfort ourselves and out of boredom. If you are feeling depressed, it is easy to use food and drink as substitutes for your normal routines and interactions. You may not feel like talking to people or going out with your friends, you may stop your regular exercise regime and your after-work activities, you may not feel like shopping and cooking for a meal, the effort may be just too much, and staying at home eating takeaway pizza and drinking alcohol seems comforting and less stressful by comparison.

But this sort of diet, if eaten regularly, is not going to enhance your mood and, coupled with lack of exercise, it might contribute to unwanted weight gain. You then risk compounding your depressive symptoms with feelings of low self-image and self-loathing for letting yourself go. Listening to dietary advice may be the last thing you feel up to, but take it slowly and don't try to change things overnight, or when you are feeling particularly down. Follow some of the simple tips on the following list because a healthier diet really will make you feel better, but don't beat yourself up if you backslide with the occasional pizza.

- Keep fruit in the house and eat a piece whenever you can.
- Don't shop when you feel particularly low and tired; you will only buy the quick-fix, sugary, fatty foods when you are feeling like this.
- If you feel like sugary snacks, try to make them whole-grain, such as flapjacks or wholewheat biscuits, then the

wholegrains will modify the sugar rush and prevent you from having extreme mood highs and lows.

- Have healthy snacks to hand, such as walnuts, almonds, dried apricots and figs, wholemeal bread, organic peanut butter, olives, salad vegetables you can munch on such as celery, baby tomatoes, cucumber, peppers. Eat half an avocado with a squeeze of lemon and some olive oil. Boil some eggs and store them in the fridge to snack on.
- When you cook, cook in bulk, so you don't have to cook the next night.
- If you have a takeaway, choose baked potato with tuna and olive oil, homemade soup and bread, Japanese sushi, vegetables with noodles. Add your own salad, oil and fruit.
- Fresh-squeezed juice is a wonderful pick-me-up. Try carrot, apple and ginger, or orange, banana and strawberry.
- For every glass of wine or spirits you drink, drink a glass of mineral water. Have some alternatives to alcohol handy, such as fresh juice which you can dilute with sparkling water to make it a bit more special.

The secret is to stock up with healthy, quick-to-prepare items to lessen the temptation of bingeing on too much of the wrong sort of food. If you can't face the supermarket, get someone else to come with you and help.

Foods We Should Eat to Maximise Our EPA and EFA Levels

Now let's look at the EFA-rich foods you should be eating in order to raise your essential fatty acid levels. By doing so you will be nurturing your brain-cell membranes to ensure a healthy, functioning brain which is less likely to become depressed. We outline the foods with the highest levels of EFAs, including those most rich in EPA, and we also mention the foods that sabotage essential fatty acids. We then go on to suggest some ways you can begin to include the healthier foods in your daily diet, and ways to reduce the less healthy options.

There are various points to consider if you are to make sure you are eating the right EPA- and EFA-rich food.

- Direct and indirect dietary sources of EPA.
- The foods with the highest levels of EPA, such as oily fish.
- How much of these foods we need every day.
- The safety issues concerning oily fish.
- Balancing omega-3 and omega-6 oils in our diet.
- Other food sources of EFAs.
- Ways to include these EFAs in our daily diet.
- How best to store and cook food to maximise their EFA levels.
- Vitamins and minerals that enhance absorption of fatty acids.
- Foods to avoid, which help block the metabolism of EFAs.

Direct and Indirect Dietary Sources of EPA

Let's start with the omega-3 family which includes EPA, the fatty acid most implicated in alleviating depression. As we have already mentioned in Chapter 4, ALA is the source essential fatty acid at the beginning of the omega-3 meta-bolic pathway, which metabolises into EPA in the diet. EPA then metabolises into DHA. There are two ways we can obtain EPA through diet. The first is by eating it directly in fish and fish oils, and smaller amounts in meat, poultry, eggs and offal. The second is by eating ALA in oils, nuts, seeds and dark green leafy vegetables, and allowing it to form EPA via the metabolic pathway. This a slower and less reliable option than eating EPA-rich foods directly, because during the process of

converting from ALA to EPA the fatty acids can be sabotaged by diet and lifestyle habits that we discuss later in the
chapter. While eating foods rich in ALA will not deliver the
same amount of EPA into the brain-cell membrane as eating
a food rich in EPA itself, ALA-rich foods are none the less
a valuable source of EPA in the diet.

Later in the chapter we explain the difference in the types
of oil – mono-, poly , and saturated – that contain these valuable EFA nutrients, and how to find the oils that are highest
in essential fatty acids and therefore best for you.

Oily fish as a dietary source of EPA

Eating oily fish is one of the best ways of obtaining EPA
through our diet. The fish with the highest levels of EPA are
cold-water fish with heavier, darker flesh such as mackerel,
salmon, herring, sardine, trout and tuna. It used to be the case
that fish was a major part of the British diet. We are an island
after all, and fish was abundant and cheap. But the modern
diet contains precious little fish, and the most popular types
that we do eat – the fish and chip suppers and fish fingers –
are cod, haddock and plaice, which are not oily fish and
therefore do not contain large amounts of omega-3 fatty
acids. Cod liver contains EPA, but we don't eat the liver in
fish fingers or fish suppers.

Now, in the light of Dr Puri's depression research, we
need to reintroduce fish into our diet to raise our levels of
dietary EPA.

How much oily fish?

If we are going to eat more fish to help raise our levels of
EPA and ward off depression, how much is enough? The
Food Standards Agency UK recommend eating one portion

of oily fish a week, which delivers around 2 grams of EFAs a week, depending on the variety and how much you cook it. This is thought to be the recommended intake to help prevent heart disease and the other EFA-related conditions mentioned above. But other scientists feel that our daily intake should be higher, at 0.5 grams of EFAs a *day*, especially if you are at risk of heart disease or suffer from arthritis.

- Canned fish has lower levels than fresh or frozen fish. For instance, raw tuna contains an average of 1.6 grams of EFA per 100 grams, whereas canned tuna only contains 0.3 grams.
- Raw fish, such as Japanese sushi, is higher in EFAs, but if you cook your fish, don't overcook it.

Cooking Suggestions

- Stir-fry strips of oily fish with fresh chopped vegetables in sesame, rapeseed or olive oil. Then drizzle uncooked oil over the finished dish.
- Grill salmon steaks and make a mayonnaise with olive oil. Serve with broccoli and wholegrain brown rice.
- Mash cooked, flaked mackerel with soft cheese, chopped chives and a teaspoon each of olive oil and sunflower oil. Add a squeeze of lemon, black pepper and a few drops of Tabasco. Spread on wholewheat toast.
- Mash tinned sardines with two teaspoons of olive oil, chopped fresh parsley and the juice of half a lemon. Make a sandwich with sliced tomato and wholewheat bread or toast.
- Add chopped walnuts, fresh sunflower oil, chopped avocado and fresh spinach leaves to a tin of tuna for a quick lunch.

Safety issues relating to fish intake

The reason the Food Standards Agency have sought to limit our fish intake to one portion of oily fish a week is because research has shown that chemicals such as PCBs (polychlorinated biphenyls) and heavy metals are polluting our seas, and so contaminating the entire fish stock.

There is ongoing research to find out whether this is old pollution from a century of industrial emissions, or whether the current emissions are the main source of the pollution. The fish that arouse most concern are the larger fish, which have had longer to accumulate these toxins in their bodies. These include shark, swordfish and marlin, which have been found to be high in methylmercury levels. Shark is not considered an oily fish, but swordfish and marlin are. And although we in Britain do not eat a lot of these Pacific Ocean fish, increasingly we are seeing swordfish and shark in fishmongers, supermarkets and restaurants.

This sounds very alarming, but government health guidelines still recommend we eat the smaller oily fish such as salmon and mackerel once a week, and in fact a healthy adult is extremely unlikely to be affected by these contaminants unless they are consumed in vast quantities. Eating salmon, mackerel, trout or sardines once or twice a week is a good and healthy addition to your diet if you follow these guidelines:

- Pregnant women, women who want to become pregnant, babies and small children are advised not to eat shark, swordfish or marlin except occasionally, as high levels of these contaminants can interfere with the functioning of the nervous system.
- Stick to the other types of oily fish, such as the more common salmon and mackerel, which do not grow to

such a large size, and have not been shown to be so affected.

- Know your fish. As it seems all fish stocks are contaminated with potentially dangerous pollutants, it is wise to know the source of the oily fish, and any other fish, you buy. A good fishmonger or supermarket will source their fish from areas of least pollution, so ask. Also avoid large, older fish of any type, whose flesh will be more likely to contain higher levels of contaminants. Fish farms have a more strictly controlled environment, so farmed salmon or trout should be less polluted.

Balancing Omega-3 and Omega-6 in Our Diet

One of the factors in getting a healthy supply of dietary EFAs is balancing the two types of EFAs, omega-3 and omega-6 fatty acids, in the food we eat. There has been some controversy in the US recently about the benefits of certain fatty acids. Doctors are concerned about the unwanted side effects of consuming too many omega-6 fatty acids and not enough omega-3. Too large a consumption of omega-6, without the balancing omega-3 fatty acid, is thought by some scientists to predispose us to fluid retention, raised blood pressure and increased blood clotting.

Although the experts are still not in agreement about what exactly is the right ratio of omega-3 to omega-6, there is general consensus that people in the UK, America and particularly Australia eat far too much omega-6 and not enough omega-3. It is said that the current ratio is between 10 and 20:1, i.e. 10 to 20 parts omega-6 to 1 part omega-3, rather than the general ideal of between 2 and 5:1.

This imbalance has come about first because of the vast increase in refined vegetable oils, such as corn and sunflower used in processed food and cooking, which contain omega-6. Second, the consumption of oily fish has fallen dramatically, so most people's omega-3 levels are low, and if they are eating oily fish, their omega-3 fatty acids are being sabotaged by too much hydrogenated fat being consumed as well.

You can find a balance by avoiding refined cooking oils and processed food such as pastry, biscuits and cakes as much as possible. Use raw, cold pressed, unrefined oil from both fatty acid chains instead and increase your intake of oily fish. If you are going to supplement your diet, choose a supplement that is a balance of both fatty acid chains.

If you are eating a healthy diet with lots of fresh food and healthy oils, you will be in no danger of consuming too much omega-6 fatty acid.

Other Foods Containing EPA and EFAs

Although oily fish is the best source of EPA, there are many other foods that are rich in EFAs, both omega-3 and omega-6. Incorporating these foods into your daily diet will help to raise your essential fatty acid levels. Although these foods do not contain such high quantities of EPA as oily fish, they are good alternatives to fish as sources of EPA and other EFAs, especially if you are a vegetarian and would not consider eating fish or fish oils, or if you are allergic to fish. EFA-rich foods include:

- Omega-3 fatty acids are found in nuts and nut oils, including walnut, flax, rapeseed, green leafy vegetables, lean meat, soya beans and pumpkin seeds. EPA can also be found in small amounts in chicken and eggs, and DHA is present in animal organ meat such as liver, kidney and brains.

- Omega-6 fatty acids are found in sunflower, sesame, olive and almond oils, nuts and seeds, evening primrose, black-currant and borage oil, and in small quantities in meat, dairy produce, eggs and seafood.

You can use these oils in cooking, in dressings or drizzled over food, and you can also eat the nuts and seeds, which are the source of these oils, as snacks or in salads. There are no hard and fast guidelines about how much of these EFA-rich foods you should consume in a day, but try increasing your intake of these foods in as many different ways as possible to give nutritional variety and boost your essential fatty acid levels.

Here are some suggestions to help you incorporate these EFA-rich foods into your daily diet.

Breakfast

Muesli: mix a handful of linseeds and a handful of sunflower seeds with some rolled oats and any dried or fresh fruit you like.

Stir a teaspoon of oil, such as rapeseed or walnut, into porridge or yoghurt.

Buy bread made with sunflower, walnut, sesame or olive oils, seeds or nuts.

Eat almond-nut butter on your toast. Or have a boiled or poached egg.

Flax Oil (Linseed) (*Linum usitatissumum*)

Flaxseed contains omega-3 and omega-6 fatty acids. Take as a medicinal oil; dosage: 1 teaspoon to 1 tablespoon of oil once or twice a day. Or you can eat the seeds, 1–2 tablespoons twice a day.

Flax oil is very unstable and goes off quickly when exposed to the air or high temperatures. Buy small amounts, store it in a dark glass bottle in the fridge, and use within six weeks of opening.

Walnut Oil (*Juglans regia*)

A great favourite in French cooking, now more popular in Britain, this oil has high level of ALA and LA. Heating oil loses most of its beneficial EFAs, so use this oil like the French, in salad dressings and sauces. Or eat the nuts in salads or as a snack. Try spinach and walnut salad with olive oil dressing.

Mid-morning

Mix a bag of raw, unsalted nuts, such as walnuts and almonds, and pumpkin seeds, and snack on them when you feel hungry.

Add a tablespoon of oil, such as rapeseed, which has no taste, to a fruit smoothie.

Eat a sesame seed bar.

Rapeseed Oil (*Brassica napus*)

This oil is used both for industrial purposes and in cooking. It is virtually tasteless but is packed with omega-3 ALA and omega-6 LA.

Sunflower Seeds and Oil (*Helianthus annuus*)

A good source of omega-6 LA, sunflower oil is popular for cooking and salad dressings. Buy the unrefined version from health-food shops and use it cold to retain the most nutrients. Store it in the fridge.

Sesame Seeds and Oil (*Sesamum indicum*)

This is a good oil to cook with, as it is more stable and less at risk of forming toxins when heated. It is a valuable source of omega-6.

Lunchtime

Make a salad of dark green leaves, walnut halves, salad vegetables of your choice and crumbled blue cheese. Make a dressing from olive, walnut or sunflower oil, lemon and herbs.

Mix a spoonful of oil, a squeeze of lemon juice and chopped herbs into some cream cheese or cottage cheese and eat either spread on bread or in a baked potato. Sprinkle with sunflower seeds or linseeds.

Eat some hummus (which is made from chickpeas and tahini paste made from sesame seeds) with vegetable strips, such as cucumber, peppers and carrot.

Drizzle olive, walnut or sesame oil on to grilled chicken and steamed vegetables with a squeeze of lemon, Tabasco and some fresh chopped herbs.

Extra Virgin Olive Oil (*Olea europea*)

This oil is a health treatment all by itself. It contains omega-6 LA and vitamin E and lowers cholesterol levels, which are linked to heart disease, at the same time as protecting the 'good' cholesterol levels, the high-density lipids, from being destroyed. This is particularly important given the link between heart disease and depression. Make sure it is the dark, cold-pressed, extra-virgin variety for maximum health benefit.

Pumpkin Seeds (*Cucurbita pepo*)

These are high in omega-3 and omega-6. A healthy anytime snack.

Suppertime

Crush some black olives with capers, anchovies and olive oil to make tapenade, which you can eat on bread or crackers.

Stir-fry vegetables and tofu with sesame oil, then drizzle a little cold sesame oil over the food before eating.

Drizzle olive, walnut or rapeseed oil cold on top of vegetable soup.

Make a mayonnaise from olive oil and egg yolks and eat with fish, chicken or lean meat. Add fresh herbs to taste.

Sprinkle chopped almonds over yoghurt and fruit.

Soya Beans (*Glycine max*)

Especially if you don't eat fish or meat, soya beans are a good source of omega-3. You can eat them in the form of soya oil, in the form of vegetable protein such as tofu, or in soya milk. Replacing some of the animal products in your diet with soya alternatives can reduce your saturated fat intake.

Almonds and Almond Oil (*Prunus amygdalus*)

Sweet almond oil is good for controlling cholesterol levels, and has a high omega-3 content. You can use it in cooking, eat the nuts whole, chopped in salads, sprinkled over yoghurt and fruit, ground in cakes and added to soups.

MEDICINAL SOURCES OF EFAS

As well as eating EFAs in food, we can obtain them from medicinal oils. Flax oil is a medicinal omega-3 oil (see above). Omega-6 medicinal oils include evening primrose, borage and blackcurrant, all of which are rich in GLA, which plays a wide variety of roles in your body's health, including maintaining cellular health and helping produce beneficial prostaglandins.

Evening Primrose Oil (*Oenothera biennis*)

This plant, native to North America, metabolises in the body to form prostaglandins, one in particular called E1, which is believed to control several critical body functions, such as the immune response to infections, blood clotting and hormonal balance. This is the best source of GLA available. Dosage: 500–1000 mg daily, usually in capsule form. Improvement in symptoms might not show for twelve weeks.

Borage Oil (*Borago officinalis*) (Starflower)

This plant extract is a good source of GLA, but the GLA from borage is less easily absorbed into the cells than evening primrose oil, so take evening primrose in preference. Dosage: 1000 mg daily, usually in capsule form.

Blackcurrant Seed Oil (*Ribes nigrum*)

Again, potentially a good source of GLA, but not as good at prostaglandin production as evening primrose. Dosage: 1500 mg daily, in capsule form.

HOW BEST TO BUY, STORE AND COOK FOOD TO MAXIMISE EFA LEVELS

High temperatures and poor storage can destroy the essential fatty acids in the food you eat, so it is best, when preparing your meals, to include a large proportion of your EFA-rich foods in their raw state. Oil, particularly, is quite unstable, and needs careful storage. There are also a lot of refined oils on the market which have lost much of their goodness in the refining process.

Here are a few tips to preserve the essential fatty acids in your food:

- Read the label carefully when buying oil. Although it is more expensive, always buy unrefined, cold-pressed, virgin oil from a reliable source.
- Make sure when you buy oil that the bottle is dark green or brown glass to protect the oil from the light. Store the oil in the fridge wherever possible, in an airtight bottle or can.
- Heating destroys EFAs, so eat nuts, seeds and oils raw as much as possible. When you do use oils for cooking, also add cold oil to the finished dish to maintain EFA nutrients.
- Eat fresh food rather than tinned food wherever possible, including oily fish.

VITAMINS AND MINERALS THAT ENHANCE ABSORPTION OF FATTY ACIDS

Certain vitamins and minerals support the absorption of EFAs in the body. Zinc, magnesium and vitamin B6 have been particularly shown to do this.

Zinc: a trace mineral vital to many body functions, such as immune system response, growth and wound healing. It also aids sex hormone function. Zinc deficiency can produce weak hair and nails, loss of taste, smell and appetite, and skin conditions such as eczema and psoriasis.

Dietary sources include: red meat, wholegrains, wheatgerm, pulses, eggs and cheese.

Side effects: none if taken in doses of up to 50 mg a day.

Magnesium: like calcium, this important metal is found in bones and teeth and interacts with calcium. It is vital in energy production, healthy nerve cell function and the metabolism of EFAs, and it helps in the production of mood chemicals such as dopamine. Magnesium deficiency is quite common, and causes tiredness, loss of appetite, muscle cramps and weakness, palpitations and low blood sugar.

Dietary sources include: wholegrains, nuts, soybean, dark green leafy vegetables, seafood, dairy products, eggs, bananas and chocolate.

Side effects: none, but should be taken with calcium supplement.

Vitamin B complex: includes vitamins B1, B2, B3, B5, B6 and B12. The B group vitamins work best when taken together and are important in metabolism, energy production and enzyme function. They also improve brain and nervous system function, so are an important influence on mood.

Dietary sources include: yeast extract, wholegrains, nuts, eggs, meat and green leafy vegetables.

Side effects: B3 and B6 can cause nerve and liver damage if taken alone in high doses.

These vitamins and minerals can also be taken in supplement form. Follow the instructions for dosage accompanying the product and always buy the best quality you can afford from a reputable company. It is also a good idea to take a good quality multivitamin supplement daily. The synergistic effect of these vitamins will help with the conversion of EFAs.

FOODS TO AVOID, WHICH HELP BLOCK THE METABOLISM OF EFAS

As we have discussed, EFAs are easily sabotaged on their path to the phospholipid layer. From the moment you eat them in your EFA-rich foods, other foods, namely saturated and trans fats and high-cholesterol foods, are helping to block these EFAs from converting into brain-enhancing components. So if you are to maintain high EFA levels in your body, there are some foods you would be wise to avoid as much as possible. Always read the labels on the food you buy, as often a seemingly healthy product, such as a nutrition bar, contains high levels of saturated fats. Of course, unless you are on a very healthy diet, you will eat these foods at times, but try to cut back as much as possible.

EFA-blocking foods include:

- Processed food. Many of the products we eat today are processed with saturated fats, such as crisps, biscuits, cakes, ready meals, soups, puddings, even some fruit drinks. Try to replace a few with some fresh-cooked alternatives that include lots of healthy nuts, seeds and oils.
- Fried food, for example chips, is cooked at very high temperatures using either refined, hydrogenated oils or saturated fats such as lard. This puts fried food high on the list of EFA-blocking foods.
- Fast food, such as pizza, curries, fish and chips and burgers, contains high levels of saturated fat. Another problem with this sort of food is that you have no way of knowing exactly how the ingredients have been stored and cooked. Junk food should only be an occasional indulgence.

Remember, no diet is going to be perfect all the time. There are occasions where you are eating out or staying with friends or family, or travelling, when you just don't have access to healthy food options. But if you get used to eating healthy EFA-rich foods most of the time, you can afford the occasional lapse.

You can also consider taking a daily high–EPA supplement which delivers the converted fatty acid, i.e. EPA, directly into your system.

LIFESTYLE FACTORS THAT AFFECT LEVELS OF EFAS IN YOUR BODY

As well as eating foods high in essential fatty acids, and making sure you avoid EFA-blocking foods as much as possible, there is another factor to take into account if you are to protect the integrity of your EFA levels and ensure optimum brain cell flexibility. This is the lifestyle factor. Foods themselves are not the only substances that block the conversion of EFAs in the body. Stress, alcohol, smoking and ageing also play a part in reducing EFA levels.

High Adrenaline (Epinephrine) Caused by Stress

Stress is extremely common in today's high-pressured society, and is a contributory factor in depression. Here's the reason why. Adrenaline is the hormone secreted by the adrenal glands in response to stress. We need this hormone for the 'fight or flight' survival mechanism, which gives us a boost of energy to save ourselves from danger, but these days it is much more often secreted in response to unwelcome everyday anxiety from the stress of modern life. When it is present in our bodies in high levels over long periods of time, it damages our body systems, and one of the systems it damages is the conversion process of EFAs. So high adrenaline levels mean low levels of EFAs.

We don't always realise it, but many of us have become used to living with stress. All stress isn't bad; we need a challenge, we need the stimulus of trying new things and pushing ourselves to achieve difficult goals, but we don't need unwelcome stress, the sort that, for instance, the electronic age has brought. Mobile phones, computers, faxes and e-mails are excellent technological advances, and we wouldn't be without them, but they have their downside too. For instance, you can't have a quiet moment anywhere, even with your friends and family, and guarantee you won't be interrupted by the screech of someone's mobile. We have learned to expect instant communication. 'Where were you? I couldn't get hold of you,' we are often told if we go 'off-line'. But for many people, never being off-line is very stressful.

Then there is the speed at which we live – always on the run, never even stopping to eat a proper meal – and the noise from overcrowded cities, piped music, traffic, car and house alarms. Or the image stress of being thin enough, or having a wrinkle-free face and firm breasts – many women have Botox treatment rather than lunch these days. Or the environmental pollution from carbon monoxide emissions, from the additives and pesticides in our food and the chemicals in our water.

Every generation has its stresses, but we seem to have more than most in our hi-tech age. We can't easily change our environment, but we can learn to deal with stress more efficiently, to avoid too much damaging adrenaline pumping around our body. Here are some tips to prevent the stress factor from reducing your levels of EFAs:

- Be realistic about what you can comfortably achieve in a day. Don't over-stretch yourself, and learn to say 'no'.

- Be organised; a lot of stress is caused by forgetting things, losing things, being late, missing deadlines and so on.
- Have proper meals. Gobbling a breakfast bar on the bus is not breakfast. Eating in front of the computer is not a lunch break.
- Drink lots of water. This helps wash toxins from your system.
- Have time to yourself when you can wind down and do what *you* want to do, whatever that is.
- Exercise. This is vital because aerobic exercise helps to burn off stress hormones. You should exercise a little every day, even if it is just walking briskly for fifteen minutes, which also has the advantage of getting you out into the fresh air and daylight. A calming, non-aerobic exercise, such as yoga, is also beneficial for letting go of tensions and relaxing the mind (see exercise section in Chapter 8).
- Meditate. Many people are nervous of meditation, thinking it is only for the spiritually enlightened. But it does not have to be difficult. There are many different meditation techniques which can help to calm the mind and give you a perspective on your life. Meditation requires practice, and it is helpful to get guidance from an expert at first, but it is worth the effort.
- Breathe properly. Most of us use only the top triangle of our lungs. This means we get inadequate oxygen to the brain, and this prevents us metabolising unwanted stress hormones. Full diaphragmatic breathing calms you down. So take a deep breath!
- Sleep well. Stress hormones can stop us sleeping, and the subsequent tiredness only stresses us more. So we need to learn sleep techniques that give us adequate rest. Avoid stimulants such as alcohol, coffee and tea, or heavy meals

late at night, make sure your bedroom is airy and comfortable, wind down before bedtime and create a routine for yourself so your body is ready for sleep.

- Have a massage. Manual massage of the body tissues helps eliminate toxins, including stress hormones, and is fantastically calming. Try to budget for a monthly massage, or more often if you can afford it.
- Try to change any elements of your life that make you unhappy. This may sound glib, but many of us just accept that we hate our job or are unhappy in our relationship without even trying to do something about it. Change may not be easy, but if it is for the better it will reduce your stress in the long term.
- Have some fun! Do things you enjoy, be it abseiling or having a drink with friends. Find time to let your hair down.

By reducing the stress in your life, you will give your essential fatty acids a better chance of reaching their desired goal in supporting your brain and body tissues.

Alcohol and EFAs

When you are depressed, it is easy to turn to alcohol as a temporary escape from your reality. But, as we have discussed in Chapter 3, this exacerbates the symptoms of depression and interferes with the treatment, as well as causing social and health problems. And on the biochemical front, alcohol is also a substance that blocks the conversion of EFAs by interfering with the metabolic pathways of the omega-3 and omega-6 fatty acid chains and preventing essential fatty acids reaching the phospholipid layer in our brain. One of the problems with drinking to excess is that your habit can increase to unhealthy levels without you being aware of what is happening. Drinking is so much part of a modern social life; if you go out with friends you are expected to drink, and can be given a very hard time if you do not.

When you are experiencing the low mood of depression, which refuses to lift, it is tempting to dull your despair by drinking more and more, until your body becomes used to these new, higher levels of alcohol and you begin to crave the next drink. This can put an even greater strain on your relationships with family, friends and work colleagues than the symptoms of the depression itself. It also puts a strain on all your body systems. Obviously people's tolerance to alcohol varies depending on your age, sex and general fitness, but one or two small glasses of wine a day is not considered damaging to your health.

If you think you might have a drink problem, ask yourself these questions:

- Do you ever feel guilty that you drink too much?
- Have other people commented on how much you drink?
- Do you drink at times of the day when other people don't, like first thing in the morning or late into the night when everyone else has gone to bed?
- Has your intake of alcohol risen noticeably recently?
- Has alcohol interfered with your work or your home life because of hangovers, bad temper or accidents?

If you have answered 'yes' to two or more, you are probably drinking more than is healthy for you, and you should consider changing your drinking habits. If need be, visit your doctor and talk to them about the problem, or try these strategies for reducing your consumption.

- Don't stock alcohol in large quantities at home. If it isn't there, you can't drink it.
- Try not to drink alone. It is easier to ignore how much you are drinking if you are alone.
- If you are meeting friends, always make the first drink a soft one, and say you will have a 'proper' one later. For many people it is that first drink that sets the tone for the evening. If you have a soft drink first, the moment passes and so does the immediate need for alcohol.
- Have a few alcohol-free days each week.
- Avoid friends who drink heavily. People who drink heavily inevitably seek out others who have the same habit, and this is often the biggest hurdle to get over when you are reducing your intake. Try to stick with your more abstemious friends.
- Drink water as well as alcohol, between drinks and particularly before going to bed to reduce the effect on your liver and help flush out the toxins more quickly.
- Never drink on an empty stomach.
- If you feel you have a serious addiction to alcohol and want to give up, contact Alcoholics Anonymous. The association has a high level of success in controlling your habit.

Smoking and EFAs

Smoking and alcohol tend to go together, and, like alcohol, smoking prevents EFAs from being metabolised properly into the phospholipids essential to brain health. We are told that after seventy-two hours without a cigarette we are no longer chemically addicted to nicotine, the addictive substance found in all tobacco. But that is not the whole story, as anyone who has had a problem giving up smoking will tell you. When you smoke you become psychologically addicted to cigarettes, not just chemically. You use smoking to calm you down, as a prop to boost your social confidence, almost as a friend. Talk to many habitual smokers and they cannot imagine their lives without cigarettes. But it is important to try to give up this habit, even if you can't manage it while you are depressed. There are *no* health benefits, and tobacco is packed with chemicals known as carcinogens, which promote cancerous growths. But you know all this and somehow it doesn't make it any easier to give up. Contact the association Action for Smoking and Health (ASH) for information and support in giving up – they have a helpline – and check out the following tips:

- It's easier to quit than to cut down. If you cut down you will find your consumption creeps back up to normal very quickly.
- Alcohol and smoking go together like peaches and cream. Try giving up both for a few weeks until your no-smoking habit is well established.
- Just because you don't buy cigarettes, don't kid yourself you don't smoke. Many people sustain a heavy smoking habit by cadging cigarettes off their friends.
- You won't quit successfully if your heart is not in it. Arm yourself with clear-cut information about the horrible things tobacco smoke can inflict on your body: cancer, heart disease, wrinkles, emphysema, low EFAs.
- Avoid smoking areas when you are giving up. Stick to non-smoking restaurants and cinemas rather than pubs. Make your home a no-smoking zone.
- Use the nicotine patches and gum to help kick-start your campaign to quit, but remember these are only aids; you need to start thinking of yourself as a non-smoker, not a smoker who wears nicotine patches.

- Remind yourself how difficult giving up is. If you start again, you'll eventually have to give up again.
- Try hypnosis; it has a high success rate if you genuinely want to quit.
- Warning! Smokers usually start again when under stress, when they think they have become non-smokers and can afford the odd cigarette, and when they are drunk.

Ageing and EFAs

Ageing is another factor that reduces our levels of EFAs. This is because all the body systems slow down as we get older, and the tissues in the body become less mobile as they age. This might explain why such a high proportion of older people suffer from depression. Obviously we can't do anything about getting older, but we can make sure that we do all we can to keep ourselves in the best possible health by following a sensible diet and exercise regime (see Chapter 8). You can also take a daily high EPA supplement to enhance EFA levels and feed the brain.

Changing the way you eat and breaking health-compromising lifestyle habits to incorporate all the healthy, EFA-promoting ideas we have detailed above will take a bit of time and commitment. We lead busy lives with little time to concentrate on such things, especially if we are depressed and not up to instigating any new activity. But the sooner you begin to create a healthier lifestyle and eating pattern, the sooner you will feel healthier and stronger, and become more resistant to minor illnesses such as colds, and major illnesses such as depression.

So make a three-pronged attack on your depression: take a daily high EPA supplement, either as treatment for or protection against depression; increase the levels of EFAs, particularly EPA, in your food; and reduce the factors in your food and diet that sabotage levels of EFAs. This is the best way to fight depressive illness both in the short and the long term.

In the next chapter we look at all the health benefits of increasing your EPA levels, i.e. the *good* side effects.

Points to Remember

- You can take a high EPA supplement, found in chemists, health-food stores and some supermarkets, to alleviate your depression symptoms.
- High EFA levels are important for general health and avoiding depression.
- Your body does not make EPA or other EFAs, you have to eat them in food or supplements.
- One of the best sources of EPA is oily fish, which should be eaten once or twice a week; alternatively take a supplement.
- Much of the food we eat, particularly saturated and trans fat, can prevent EFAs from converting into the phospholipids essential to brain health and the absence of depression.
- Not all fat is bad. Healthy oils such as flax, olive and walnut are full of EFAs, but convenience food tends to be full of fats that block EFAs.
- Lifestyle habits such as smoking and heavy drinking also compromise the conversion of EFAs in your body.
- Avoid stress, or learn how to cope with it. Stress lowers fatty acid levels in the body.
- Your diet and lifestyle will never be perfectly healthy, but start making improvements now to raise the levels of EFAs in your system.

Chapter Seven

Everyone Can Benefit from EPA

We have discussed the stunning benefits EPA has in the treatment of depression, but there is other good news, which is not just for depression sufferers: EPA has a much wider application, with research showing that it can act to improve and protect our day-to-day health, and also offer hope to sufferers of a diverse range of diseases including heart disease, arthritis and Huntington's disease.

This chapter details all the general benefits that result from taking EPA, and is important for anyone, no matter how young or old, who is not currently ill, but who wants to improve their overall health, their brain function and their hair and skin condition, as well as protect themselves from disease in the future. We also explain the particular medical conditions that are now beginning to be successfully treated with EPA, and the research that has prompted these exciting advances in treatment.

The reason why EPA has such a multi-purpose application is because essential fatty acids work at such a fundamental level in the body, nurturing and mobilising the core of the cell membrane, which in turn enhances all the body systems. If your body systems are functioning at optimum health, you will suffer less from disease, and any disease you are currently experiencing, such as depression, can be treated more successfully. This means that you do not have to be suffering from a depressive episode to take a regular, daily EPA supplement. It makes sense for us all, depression sufferers and non-depression sufferers alike, to increase our EPA and EFA levels, and so take advantage of the general benefits of this amazing health discovery.

The Benefits of EPA for Everyone

We all want to look and feel our best but, as we discussed in Chapter 6, even if, on the whole, we eat a reasonably healthy diet and don't indulge in too many destructive lifestyle habits such as drinking and smoking to excess, most of us still lead high-pressure, quite stressful lives with erratic eating habits and lack of exercise for periods of time. We may be trying to bring up a family and work full-time, or we may have a high-powered job that demands long hours and a lot of travelling, or we may be going through life traumas such as divorce or bereavement, coping with a sick relative, or simply getting old. It's life, and even those of us who are most dedicated to a healthy lifestyle cannot always pay attention to our physical health and wellbeing. So it makes sense to get all the help we can to maintain our bodies in their optimum condition and ward off the diseases that are associated with stress and a run-down system. Let's look at some of the ways EPA can help us all to look and feel healthy and well.

A HEALTHIER HEART

We all understand the importance a healthy heart has in our general health. If our heart is unhealthy, all the systems in our body are compromised because of the reduced circulation of blood, carrying oxygen and other nutrients to the various organs. Contributory factors to heart disease include drinking too much alcohol, smoking, eating a high saturated fat diet and failing to exercise regularly; it is important to avoid these factors, but it has now been found that omega-3 fish oils such as EPA can improve the health of your heart.

Here are some of the benefits to your heart of taking fish oils or a vegetarian high EPA supplement:

- Fish oils, such as EPA, act on the blood as an anticoagulant. This means that they thin the blood. This is a huge advantage to us all, because our increasingly saturated fat diet has meant that our arteries are becoming clogged by unwanted fatty deposits, such as the 'bad' type of cholesterol. These fats narrow the arteries and restrict the blood flow, making the likelihood of clots forming in any of the major arteries a real health problem. If a clot forms in the arteries around the heart, you will suffer a heart attack. So high levels of essential fatty acids greatly reduce the risk of heart attacks by keeping the blood flowing more smoothly and reducing its tendency to clot (see Taking Anticoagulants box, p. 189).
- Fish oils enhance the production of red blood cells, which carry oxygen round the body. Oxygen is vital for the healthy function of all the organs in the body. This is why exercise is so important, because it increases your heart rate, making the blood, and therefore the oxygen, move more quickly through the body.

- Fish oils lower unhealthily high blood pressure by ensuring the smooth flow of blood in the arteries and reducing strain on the heart. This is good news because the current drugs used to lower blood pressure all have, like antidepressants, a worrying list of side effects. These can include impotence, headaches and drowsiness. But if you are currently on anti-hypertensive drugs, *do not stop taking them without consulting your doctor.* This is very important, as sudden withdrawal can send your blood pressure rocketing up. Take a high EPA supplement alongside your antihypertensive drug at first, then gradually reduce your medication under professional super-vision if your blood pressure responds to the supplement.
- Fish oils and vegetarian high EPA supplements help control irregular heart beats, known as cardiac arrhythmia, by improving blood flow to the heart. Arrhythmia can be a cause of heart attacks.
- Taking a high EPA supplement can help prevent heart disease, just as it helps prevent depression. So even if you are not currently suffering from heart problems, it still makes sense to increase your intake of oily fish, or take a high EPA supplement daily.

If you are depressed, taking a fish oil supplement is impor-tant for your heart as well as your depression, it seems, as studies have shown there to be a curious link between depres-sion and heart attacks, and there is some evidence to suggest that becoming depressed may often predict the possibility of a heart attack. Although these findings have been replicated in a number of studies, there is no obvious reason why depres-sion should increase heart attack risk, but it makes sense to keep both depression and heart disease at bay by increasing your intake of EPA.

Taking Anticoagulants

The anticoagulant action of EFAs was first discovered by Dr Hugh Sinclair in the 1950s when he studied the blood clotting time of a group of Eskimos. Eskimos eat a mainly fish diet, so their levels of EFAs, particularly EPA, are natu rally very high. He discovered that their clotting time was significantly longer than is found in Western populations, and that the Inuit people have little experience of heart attacks.

This is why those of you taking anticoagulant drugs such as heparin or warfarin, which are commonly prescribed drugs after a heart attack, should not take an EPA supplement at the same time as your anticoagulants. If you do, you risk making your clotting time too long, which could lead to problems if you are injured and your blood clots too slowly. If you are on anticoagulants and you would prefer to take an EPA supplement, either because you are suffering from depression, or because you would prefer a more natural treatment to increase your clotting time, consult your doctor about gradually reducing your anti-coagulants and supplementing with EPA.

Do not stop taking your anticoagulants, or begin taking EPA with anticoagulants, without medical supervision.

THE BENEFITS OF EPA FOR OTHER CARDIOVASCULAR CONDITIONS

There are other conditions that stem from unwanted blood clotting that have also been shown to benefit from treatment with EPA. These include:

- **Stroke.** For the same reasons as EPA or high EPA essential fatty acids reduce the risk of heart attacks, so too do they reduce the risk of you suffering a stroke. Stroke usually occurs when one of the arteries in the brain has a blood clot, and the area of the brain supplied by that artery is damaged by the loss of its normal blood supply. This results in loss of the functions, such as speech or mobility, which that area of the brain governs. This happens increasingly as you get older, when, as we discussed in Chapter 6, your body cells are less mobile, making the tissue of your arteries less elastic and your blood cells more inclined to clump and clot, especially if you have a diet high in saturated fats.

- **Economy Class Syndrome.** This is a relatively newly identified syndrome which can occur when you travel long distances cramped up in the 'economy' section of an aeroplane, with no room to move your limbs. When this happens, the blood flow in your veins is restricted and therefore slows down, and the natural tendency of the blood to clot is increased. This is known as a deep vein thrombosis (DVT). When you then get up from your plane seat at the end of a long flight, any clot that has formed in your leg can come loose and travel through the veins to your heart or lungs, causing a potentially fatal blockage. High levels of EPA greatly reduce this risk.

To improve your heart and circulatory health and avoid succumbing to all forms of heart disease, take 500 mg of EPA in supplement form on a daily basis. Taken regularly, this will greatly benefit your heart.

HEALTHY SKIN AND HAIR

The Western world has become obsessed with looks and body image, and unfortunately most of us cannot help buying into this obsession to some extent. But with so many of us on low-fat diets, and not eating enough healthy, EFA-rich oils, the problem of dry, lacklustre, wrinkled skin has become a common Western obsession. This is because when your body is deficient in HUFAs, it first shows in your skin and hair, which also explains why one of the accompanying effects of depression is that you begin to look less healthy. Your skin loses its glow, your hair becomes dull.

We all want to look our best, and have glowing skin and healthy, shiny hair, and the cosmetics industry is quite sensibly making a fortune from this insecurity about our complexions, touting 'miracle' creams which often cost the earth, or interference from Botox or collagen injections. But a much cheaper and more successful skin treatment than those offered by the cosmetics industry is attacking the problem from the inside, because it has been shown in research trials that EFAs, particularly the omega-6 fatty acids, such as GLA found in evening primrose oil (EPO), have beneficial effects on both skin and hair.

Taking a high EPA supplement daily and increasing the healthy oils in your diet will make your skin less dry and flaky and give it a youthful glow. You will be delighted by the difference boosting your essential fatty acid levels has on your complexion. It will also remove any dandruff problems, leaving your hair strong and more shiny. Psoriasis, which is a skin condition where the skin cells over-produce leading to itching and scaliness, has also been shown to respond well to omega-3 fish oil supplements. EFAs improve skin and hair quality by increasing the normal oils that make the skin soft and smooth, reducing moisture loss from the skin and keeping the outer layer of skin, known as the epithelium, soft and youthful. Healthier skin and hair are an excellent confidence-boosting side effect of taking an EPA supplement for your depression, or as part of your general health regime.

BETTER VISION

Fatty acids play a vital role in how well we see. The retina – the layer of light-sensitive cells at the back of the eye – has the highest percentage of DHA of any organ in the body. Studies show that supplementing with omega-3 EFAs can maintain healthy vision, protect against macular degenerative disease (MDD) – the most common cause of blindness in old people – and also improve night vision. As old people are one of the groups more susceptible to depressive illness, and because degenerating vision can be a trigger for isolation and depression, here is another reason to increase your intake of essential fatty acids.

HEALTHY HORMONE BALANCE

At least 80 per cent of women of reproductive age experience some problems associated with their monthly period. The symptoms are mild for many, but for around 30–40 per cent they can be severe, meaning that these women spend a lot of their reproductive life plagued by hormonal imbalances which can cause quite serious disruptions to their home and work routines. Some women suffer from severe period pains which mean they have to take a day off work each month, and which can have serious consequences if an important event such as an exam falls on such a day. Some will have premenstrual syndrome (PMS), which can make them irritable, tired and unable to function as well as they normally would for sometimes up to four days before each monthly period. PMS can also include breast pain (mastalgia) in the run-up to each period. And at the end of a woman's reproductive years, menopause can also cause problems with hot flushes and sleepless nights.

In general, the many, often distressing symptoms of female hormone imbalance have not yet been successfully addressed by conventional medicine. However, EPA and high EFA supplementation have been shown to have a beneficial effect on these symptoms. This is because the body metabolises EFAs into hormone-like substances called prostaglandins that help regulate body processes such as the menstrual cycle. If there are low levels of EFAs in the body, these processes are impaired and the symptoms of hormonal imbalance can occur.

In several studies, women who experience mastalgia as a PMS symptom have been shown to have high levels of saturated fat in their blood and low levels of HUFAs. Saturated fats exacerbate the effect oestrogens have on breast tissue, making the breast more sensitive to hormone levels. Unsaturated fats do the opposite, making breast tissue less sensitive to hormone levels.

Dr Puri discovered that PMS responded well to EPA when treating a patient called Alison for schizophrenia. Not only did her schizophrenic symptoms disappear when she was taking EPA, but so too did the mastalgia that had plagued her for more than twenty years. The case study also highlights the attendant benefits to Alison in improving the condition of her skin and hair. Here is Dr Puri's account.

ALISON'S STORY

Alison is a forty-four-year-old librarian who was diagnosed as suffering from schizophrenia many years ago. While suffering from a particularly severe psychotic episode of the illness, about ten years ago, Alison thought that the devil and some of his demons were spying on her and trying to tempt her. As a committed Christian, she found these thoughts very troubling. Even worse, from time to time she could hear them talking about her in a derogatory way, referring to her as being profane. A typical comment might be: 'Alison's a whore.' One evening, Alison thought that their voices appeared to be coming from the lights in her room. In an attempt to stop these demonic characters (and to put an end to their voices), she grabbed hold of one of the light bulbs in both hands, and held on until the voices diminished. The light bulb was switched on during this time, and had been for several hours before, and so, unfortunately, both hands were badly burned. They required plastic surgery, including skin grafts. To this day, they no longer look normal (at least not to the trained medical eye). For example, small hairs now grow out of the skin that was grafted on to her palms.

In spite of treatment with antipsychotic drugs (which are used in the treatment of schizophrenia), Alison kept experiencing symptoms of schizophrenia, including feeling strange and believing she was being persecuted. She was referred to me by her psychiatrist. I decided to add, to her pre-existing conventional anti-schizophrenia medication, 2 grams purified ethyl-EPA per day (see Chapter 6).

Within three months, all her schizophrenia symptoms had entirely disappeared. But what was also particularly interesting was that two physical changes occurred over that three-month period. First, her scars seemed to look much better; she commented that her skin and hair had never looked so good since her teenage years. The other change was that, for the first time in her life, she stopped suffering from premenstrual syndrome (or premenstrual tension), which gave her severe breast pain each month. 'This is the first time in twenty years that I've been free of this,' she explained to me. This freedom from premenstrual syndrome has continued ever since, and Alison is absolutely delighted with the EPA treatment. She remains symptom-free.

BETTER ANTENATAL AND POSTNATAL HEALTH FOR MOTHER AND BABY

Women often worry about their own health and that of their unborn baby when they are pregnant. And because the baby takes vital nutrition directly from its mother while in the womb, it is an important time for women to be as healthy and well-fed as possible. All the issues surrounding reproduction, such as the baby's development in the womb, the mother's health, breast-feeding and problems with postnatal depression, have been shown to benefit from supplementation with EPA to ensure high levels of EFAs in a woman's body. Here's why:

- EFAs are vital for proper development of the brain and eyes of the growing foetus. In the last three months of pregnancy, brain and nervous system growth of the foetus is accelerated, so it is essential at this time to have a good supply of EFAs in your body.
- After your baby is born, EPA supplementation is important in order to prevent postnatal depression.
- The growing baby is thought to scavenge its mother's supply of essential fatty acids to make sure of its own supply while in the womb. So during pregnancy and postnatally, you

will need to replenish the stocks of EFAs that your baby has scavenged in the womb.

- If you are breast-feeding, you should maintain a high level of EFAs to enhance your baby's general health and brain development. Breast-fed babies have been shown to score, on average, eight points higher in IQ tests than bottle-fed babies.
- There is some recent research that suggests that babies who suffer Sudden Infant Death Syndrome have low levels of HUFAs in their brain.

Supplementation with EFAs during pregnancy and postnatally is both safe and beneficial to your baby's development. Follow the recommendations for pregnant women on the supplement packet for optimum dosage.

HEALTHY BONES AND JOINTS

Keeping your bones and joints healthy as you get older can be quite a problem for many people. Stiffness and joint pain from general wear and tear, aside from specific diseases such as rheumatoid or osteoarthritis, are responsible for most of the immobility that old people, and even middle-aged people, experience. And it is often the biggest problem older people face in looking after themselves. If you can't move easily it is difficult getting to the shops, you might find stairs a problem, or even just getting up in the morning. Exercise greatly benefits joint mobility, but so, it has now been discovered, does a high, daily dose of EPA.

Studies into bone and joint health, which have centred on research into rheumatoid arthritis – the inflammatory disease where joints become painful, swollen and stiff – have shown that omega-3 fish oil supplements, such as EPA, have considerable impact on joint health. Rheumatoid arthritis affects around one in a hundred adults, and can even occur in adolescents. If the affected joints are weight-bearing, such as the hips, knees or ankles, the person may have trouble walking and getting about without severe pain. Eventually deformities occur in the joints.

Colleagues of Dr Puri, working in Spain in 2000, found that, in this painful and debilitating disorder, the synovial fluid, which surrounds the joints, cushioning them from damage and helping to make them mobile, was deficient in omega-3 fatty acids. They also checked the blood plasma of these arthritis sufferers, and discovered it was deficient in EPA. These findings, coupled with the knowledge of how EFAs nurture normal bone and cartilage, and the fact that fish oils and other EFAs such as GLA contain substances that reduce inflammation and reduce tissue damage, suggest that EPA or an EFA supplement such as cod liver oil or evening primrose oil might be a successful treatment for this kind of inflammatory condition.

Numerous trials have backed up this suggestion, showing that taking a high-dose EPA and DHA supplement instead of anti-inflammatory medication produces a marked reduction in symptoms of morning pain, stiffness and tenderness when the supplement had been taken for at least three months. Dr Puri has also heard anecdotal proof of this treatment success. Many of his patients have expressed relief from joint pain as a side effect of their depression treatment with EPA. So this supplement can reduce the need for anti-inflammatory drugs, which people with rheumatoid arthritis often take for the rest of their life, plagued by their attendant side effects.

If you are currently suffering from rheumatoid arthritis, you could help reduce the severity of your symptoms by using an EFA supplement. Genulex cream, which contains EPA and DHA, would be ideal for this. It needs to be rubbed into the joints three times daily (see resource section for details). Or take a very high dose of a fish oil supplement: experts suggest 6000 mg a day in three separate doses. You can take these supplements alongside your painkillers until the effects of the supplement kick in.

The overwhelming evidence of the research studies mentioned above adds up to a concrete reason for all of us, whatever our current state of health, to begin taking an EPA supplement daily to stay as healthy and disease-free as possible. Modern medicine, with its increasingly integrated approach to combining drugs with complementary holistic therapies such as acupuncture, is no longer just about curing an existing disease. More and more it is about taking care of our overall health and wellbeing in order to *prevent* disease in the future. And EPA, with its wide-ranging health benefits, must surely be the supplement of choice for everyone.

TREATING OTHER MEDICAL CONDITIONS WITH EPA

We have dealt with the benefits of taking an EPA supplement for everyone who is currently healthy and not suffering from any disease, and for those who are depressed. But there are others too, people currently suffering from certain medical conditions for which recent research has shown EPA to be an exciting new treatment option, who can also benefit from this supplement. These are diseases which have so far not been successfully managed with conventional medical treatments, such as schizophrenia, Huntington's disease and attention deficit hyperactivity disorder, and when treatment is offered, it is often with drugs that have problematic side effects. EPA now offers real hope for sufferers of all these conditions.

Treating Schizophrenia

Schizophrenia was, as we have mentioned, the first mental disorder to be tested with EFA supplementation, which was found to be effective. People with this condition spend a lifetime on antipsychotic drugs, which, as Alison's case study above shows, are not always successful, and also, for many sufferers, have unpleasant side effects. As a result of the difficulty in finding an adequate drug to treat their symptoms, schizophrenic patients have to be constantly monitored by a doctor to make sure their symptoms are under control. Dr Puri and his colleagues' breakthrough in the treatment of this condition with pure EPA now offers hope for thousands of sufferers and the people close to them who have been witness to this debilitating condition.

Treating Chronic Fatigue Syndrome (CFS)

Another distressing and little understood disease that affects an increasing number of people in the West is CFS, also known as myalgic encephalomyelitis (ME). This complex and controversial illness is characterised by a number of variable symptoms, including feelings of intense fatigue, muscle and joint pain, depression, poor concentration, disrupted sleep patterns and headaches.

There are thought to be around a quarter of a million sufferers of this condition, which mainly affects women aged between twenty-five and forty-five, in the UK alone. There is no definitive cause for CFS; possible triggers such as viruses and personal trauma have been blamed, and there seems to be a link with depression, although it is not clear which comes first, depression or CFS. Many in the medical profession have been reluctant to see the illness as anything but a psychosomatic reaction to unhappy life circumstances, and encouraged their patients to 'pull themselves together', which will sound familiar to many depression sufferers.

But Dr Puri and his colleagues at the Hammersmith Hospital did a research study on the brains of CFS sufferers, the results of which were published in 2002. They scanned the patients' brains with an MRI scanner, using a revolutionary technique called magnetic resonance spectroscopy, and found a clear and significant chemical abnormality in these CFS patients, which they didn't find in the control group. So there was a real chemical marker for chronic fatigue syndrome. But what did this actually mean? Dr Puri consulted some colleagues who were experts in interpreting magnetic resonance spectroscopy. They told him that the results implied an abnormality in the phospholipid layer, the same problem that had been found in people with depression. Which meant that patients with CFS should, like depression sufferers, respond well to treatment with EPA.

Dr Puri also discovered that his other colleague, Professor Horrobin, had already done a trial testing high EPA supplementation as a treatment for CFS as far back as 1990, although the study, despite finding that the supplement successfully alleviated a wide range of symptoms in the people tested, was not given much attention at the time. Dr Puri went on to test his findings on his own patients, and here is his case study.

HELEN'S STORY

Helen is a twenty-eight-year-old lady who had suffered from depressed mood, persistent debilitating fatigue, muscle pains, extreme tiredness and generalised aches and pains for nine years, following a bout of a nasty flu-like illness which occurred while she was a student at university. At that time she was diagnosed as suffering from postviral fatigue syndrome, now more commonly known as chronic fatigue syndrome (CFS) or myalgic encephalomyelitis (ME). Her doctor was unsure how to treat her; certainly, no treatment she received made any difference to her symptoms.

She was referred to me in 2002. Having confirmed the diagnosis of chronic fatigue syndrome, I arranged for a number of special investigations to be carried out, which pointed to a specific type of essential fatty acid deficiency. In order to treat this, an essential fatty acid supplement rich in EPA was 'prescribed'.

Within three months Helen became well again for the first time in nine years. She now has much more energy, no depressive symptoms, and no muscular aches or chronic fatigue. She continues to take the high EPA nutritional supplement and continues to be well; she has suffered no adverse side effects from this.

As you can see from Dr Puri's case study, EPA is a successful treatment option for patients with CFS symptoms. As this disease has had so many problems with diagnosis and recognition, and, until now, most sufferers have had either to take drugs to treat individual symptoms, or have been left to try alternative therapies to find relief – none of which has been consistently successful – EPA is a significant and exciting breakthrough in this difficult disease.

Treating Attention Deficit Hyperactivity Disorder (ADHD)

ADHD is an increasing problem for children and adolescents in Western societies, and the condition, known as a hyperkinetic disorder, affects everyone associated with a child sufferer, as well as the child himself, both at home and at school. In the UK as many as 1 in every 1000 school-age children is a victim. In the US that number is much higher, at 30–50 in every 1000 children. Experts believe this is primarily a result of the high level of junk food American children consume, and we in the UK are probably not too far behind in the junk-food nightmare.

ADHD is a series of behavioural problems which fall under these headings:

- Inattention. The child will be unable to concentrate or pay attention, frequently flitting from one activity to another and never finishing any of them.
- Hyperactivity. The child will be restless, running and jumping around a lot, noisy and very talkative.
- Impulsiveness. The child will be disinhibited with people, reckless and defiant of any rules.

The most common drug treatment for this hyperkinetic disorder is a psychostimulant drug called Ritalin. Alarmingly, this drug has become one of the most frequently prescribed drugs for children in Western countries. There are some schools in America where children have to line up each day to receive their dose, but there are many unpleasant and worrying side effects associated with Ritalin, including sleep and appetite disturbance and stunted growth. Withdrawal symptoms, if a child has taken this drug for a long time, include depression and lethargy. Obviously it is far from ideal to dose young children with such powerful medication.

Dr Puri, together with one of the world's leading experts in the field of fatty acids and disorders such as ADHD, Dr Alex Richardson, theorised that EPA might work in treating this disorder. Testing the theory in 2002 with a pilot study of an EPA-containing fatty acid supplement as treatment for dyslexic children who also suffered from ADHD, they had some astonishing results. The ADHD symptoms improved after just three months in about half the group, and it turned out, when the double-blind restrictions of the trial were removed, that this half was made up of the children who had been given the EPA-containing fatty acid supplement.

This breakthrough could have a significant effect on the thousands of children affected by a disease which has such an unfortunate impact on the sufferer's ability to learn and to integrate into society. Children who have this condition can find their whole childhood blighted by their inability to respond normally. Treatment with EPA will also mean that the affected children will not experience months or even years on drugs that potentially have such damaging side effects. And continued supplementation with EPA will prevent ADHD from returning in the future, in the same way as it does with depression. It is well worth adding a high EPA supplement to your child's diet if they show signs of this disorder. Teenagers have also been shown to benefit from taking a fish oil supplement, which appears to reduce their aggressive behaviour.

Relief from Complications of Diabetes Mellitus

Diabetes mellitus, where the pancreas produces insufficient levels of the hormone insulin, or the body cells become unable to react to the hormone, can also benefit from EFA supplementation. This is very good news, as the incidence of type 2 diabetes is on the increase in the West, with around 3 million Britons currently suffering from the disease. One of the complications of this disorder if it goes untreated, or does not respond to treatment, is a problem with the nervous system known as peripheral neuropathy. This can mean tingling and numbness in the fingers and toes, which can progress to weakness, sharp pains or loss of feeling in the legs, resulting in ulcers if a minor injury goes unnoticed. Fortunately, research trials have shown that the symptoms of peripheral neuropathy are greatly improved by taking an EFA supplement which nourishes the nerve cells in the brain and the body.

Anyone suffering from diabetes has to be careful with their health so as to avoid the possible complications of the disease if the blood sugar is not controlled on a regular basis, which include heart disease as well as peripheral neuropathy. As essential fatty acids have been shown to benefit both these conditions, it makes sense for anyone suffering from diabetes to begin supplementing with EPA, and so help protect their long-term health.

EPA has been shown to protect the healthy from developing disease, and also acts as a successful treatment option for those who are suffering from a number of chronic medical conditions. So whatever your current health status, you can benefit by adding a high EPA supplement to your daily diet and can soon look forward to healthier skin and hair, more mobile joints, a healthier heart with less chance of heart attacks and strokes, and, if you are already ill and despairing of current medical treatment for your disease, you can begin to hope.

EPA is not a miracle cure for all ills, but a substance that addresses the health of all the cells in your body at a very fundamental level, and therefore helps every system in the brain and body to function at optimum efficiency. All disease, including depression, is a malfunction in one of these systems, and if one body system is malfunctioning it can throw all the others out of kilter. EPA can help nourish those systems back to health.

In the concluding chapter we take a look back at the themes of the book and how EPA has become such an important supplement in the treatment of depressive illness. We also offer a three-stage plan to support you through the different phases you may experience as you recover from depression.

Points to Remember

- You don't have to be ill to gain the health benefits of EPA.
- EPA is an effective treatment for many chronic medical conditions.
- EPA is a natural treatment which can help you reduce your dependency on long-term medication for these chronic conditions.
- EPA helps you to look good as well as feel good.
- EPA can help prevent disease as well as treat it.
- EFAs are important for your children's health, both inside the womb, during breast-feeding, and if your child suffers from conditions such as ADHD.
- EPA supports all the brain and body systems so that they can function with optimum efficiency.
- Our long-term health is a very important goal for all of us. Taking EPA is one of the ways we can achieve this goal.

Chapter Eight

Your Journey to Recovery

It is a great moment when scientists, who have followed their instincts with years of hard research, finally come up with a real success story like that of EPA and depressive illness. Depression is one of the most talked about diseases of the modern world, not just because the number of people suffering from it is growing at such an alarming rate, nor because it is an illness that causes such a high degree of unwarranted shame and disruption to the person experiencing it, but because of the publicity surrounding the plethora of modern antidepressant drugs that have flooded the market in the last decade. Drugs that, in many cases, do help depression, but of which the public have become increasingly nervous as the extent of their potential side effects becomes clear.

EPA is about to change all this. For the first time ever, and this can hardly be overstated, we have a natural substance that successfully treats depression, and which can also ensure that your depressive symptoms do not return in the future. Depression, as we have already discussed, is a complex disease, triggered by a number of contributory factors. But Dr Puri has discovered the root biochemical cause of the disease — low levels of EPA — and has shown through his and his colleagues' extensive research and clinical application that people who take this supplement in high doses can regenerate the grey matter of their brain and remove depressive symptoms. This regeneration, which comes about from the nourishment that essential fatty acids provide for the brain cells, has also been found to be the basis for EPA's success in treating other chronic health problems — diseases that hitherto have not been successfully addressed by modern medicine. All in all, the discovery of EPA is an intensely valuable contribution to helping us keep healthy both now and in the future.

Now that you understand what EPA is, how Dr Puri came to discover it as a treatment for depression, what it can do for you, and how you can gain relief from your symptoms with this natural substance, this final chapter offers a wider picture of the whole course, from beginning to end, that a depressive illness might take. We explain coping strategies for dealing with the effect this illness might have had on you, the sufferer, and on those close to you at work and at home, taking you through a three-stage plan for your recovery. Armed with this plan, you can progress confidently through the three stages, from waiting for EPA to work for you, to noticing the first signs of recovery, until you finally reach the last stage: full recovery.

Recovering from Your Depression

Of course, finding a successful treatment for your depression, such as EPA, is your first and most important practical consideration when you experience a depressive episode. But there are other factors in the process of depression that also need to be addressed. These factors relate to how this debilitating disease has affected your emotional and social welfare. With an ordinary illness you feel ill, consult a doctor, receive treatment, explain to those around you about your medical problem and get sympathy, then in most cases you recover quite quickly. Naturally there is an emotional cost to any illness; the realisation that we are vulnerable to disease can often be unsettling, and many of us find it hard to be dependent on others, even for a short time. But our approach to the average disease is largely mechanical.

Depression is different. Seeking help, diagnosis and treatment is often delayed or, as we have seen with a large proportion of depression sufferers, absent. Added to which, recovery is not immediate, it happens in stages, and even when you have recovered, it sometimes takes a while to feel truly yourself again and to regain your confidence in life. So this particular illness can have an emotional fallout not associated with other conditions. During the course of your depression you may have alienated some of the people close to you. This will depend on your circumstances, obviously, but, for instance, if you have been depressed for a while without realising it, if you have turned to alcohol or drugs to 'medicate' your distress, or if you have refused to get help even when others have suggested it, you might have a few bridges to mend now that you are recovering. But the good news is that there are lots of strategies you can employ to ease your path through the course of recovery from your depressive episode and find your way back to health and wellbeing. Here is the three-stage recovery plan.

STAGE 1. WAITING FOR EPA TO WORK FOR YOU

There is inevitably a period after you begin treatment with EPA before the fatty acid supplement has the chance to work on your symptoms. This will probably be a matter of weeks, but during this time you will continue to feel depressed. So how can you best cope with this early stage in your recovery?

- Take charge. The chances are that you will already be feeling more positive about your condition, even if the symptoms themselves are still distressing, simply because you have accepted that you are depressed and have sought help in alleviating your illness. This means that, unless you are severely depressed, you will no longer be in that bewildered state of mind that can only ask: 'What's happening to me?' You know what is happening to you, you can be confident that help is at hand, and you know that the prognosis is good. If you haven't yet begun treatment with a high EPA supplement, now is the time to do so, or consult your doctor for treatment with pure ethyl-EPA.
- Seek support. This is a very important factor in your recovery. People who suffer from depression often tend to be the sort who beat themselves up about not being able to cope. This is one of the reasons why they don't seek help, they feel they should be able to manage on their own. But you can't always manage on your own, and you have to start learning to ask for help and accepting it when it's offered. So now is the time to talk through your problem with family and close friends if you have not already done so. You can admit how you have really been feeling, and enlist their support for the weeks ahead. They will be as relieved as you are that you

have addressed your illness and are recovering. You can also explain that you are probably not going to be back to your normal self quite yet. This will help them to be understanding and patient.

- Admitting to suicidal thoughts. If your depression has given you thoughts of suicide, now is the time to own up to them. This is not always easy to do because the thoughts are very frightening and you may feel ashamed of thinking in this way, even though it is a symptom of the illness just as a rash or a headache might be a symptom of other illnesses. But you need to protect yourself from harm until the EPA begins to alleviate this depressive symptom. Those close to you will be alarmed and can sometimes be angry if you admit to wanting to kill yourself. They can see it as the ultimate selfishness. But if you can explain these feelings in terms of a rash or a headache, they should be more understanding. Try not to spend a lot of time alone if you are feeling this way, and if you feel you cannot speak to your family or friends the Samaritans are an excellent agency for people in your situation. The counsellors are trained to deal openly, non-judgementally and, above all, anonymously with you, and will support you until you feel stronger. They are available twenty-four hours a day.
- Be kind to yourself. Now is the time for treats. If you are still working, take a week off. Allow yourself indulgences, such as a good body massage, a natural therapy (see below), a day in the country to get some sunlight and fresh air, an afternoon nap, or merely a day sitting at home doing nothing at all, but not feeling guilty about it. If you had broken your leg you would not be expected to go jogging or mow the lawn; well, you don't have to do these things either, not yet. You will feel better soon.

- Avoid stress. Now is not the time to be entering into any stressful situation. You will still be feeling tired and run down, so don't take on too much. Don't accept a part in the local panto, don't change jobs or move house unless you have to, and give the marathon a miss this year. It is sometimes hard not to give in to pressure put on you by others, but this is your life, and you need proper recovery time.

- Take your addictions in hand. As heavy drinking and drug abuse can often accompany depressive episodes as a means – not usually successful – of obtaining false comfort and temporarily dulling your feelings of despair, now that you are on the road to recovery it is time to take these addictions in hand. The effects of EPA are going to be compromised in the face of large quantities of toxic substances in your body. As your depression lifts, hopefully you will feel less inclined to substance abuse, but often these habits die hard. You might need help to wean yourself off alcohol or drugs. If so, Alcoholics Anonymous or Narcotics Anonymous are both very nurturing and supportive.

- Make sure you take your EPA supplement as recommended. One of the main problems in treating depression is getting the depressed person to take their medication regularly. This is often to do with the fact that the side effects are unpleasant, but you don't need to worry about this with EPA. However, just because it is a supplement and not a heavyweight drug does not mean you can be casual about when you take it and how much. Keeping up the recommended dose is vital to your recovery.

These strategies will help you to hold on, in the weeks ahead, until your treatment begins to take effect.

STAGE 2. WHEN EPA STARTS TO TAKE EFFECT

Within a few weeks, your depressive symptoms will begin to disappear. There will be stages of improvement, but perhaps the first thing you will notice is that you no longer feel that overwhelming despair. The day ahead may not fill you full of enthusiasm yet, but you can see a chink in the blackness. This is such a great feeling, because hope in the future is so important to our lives, it is what motivates all our actions. And now you are beginning to feel less depressed, you can employ the next level of your recovery strategies.

- Find a routine again. Routine is one of the casualties of depression. When you are depressed, your life gets completely out of kilter. This is because you become so lethargic and hopeless that you cannot face normal everyday tasks, your concentration is poor so even the tasks you do attempt take an inordinately long time to complete, or you can't complete them at all, and you are probably not sleeping properly. Your life has become chaotic, especially if you live alone. For instance, you can't sleep at night, so you get up late. You can't be bothered to do housework, so your home gradually gets messier, you have no clean clothes and you lose things you need, like keys and bills that need to be paid, and the rubbish piles up. You have no decent food in the house because you can't face your weekly shop, so you don't eat breakfast. Messages on the answer-machine are mounting, but you're not in the mood to talk to friends. You forget to pay the milkman and newsagent, and the milk and paper get cancelled. You arrive at work late, hungry and looking harassed and dishevelled.

This chaos just confirms your feelings of low self-worth. But now you are on the mend, try and re-establish some of your normal routines. Don't push yourself to be fully functional yet, but begin to set yourself realistic goals, such as getting up at the same time every day, tidying up the worst of the clutter, making sure you eat regularly and nutritiously. If you feel you aren't coping with all this, ask a close friend to help you get some order back into your life.

- Don't rush back to work. If you have had time off work for your depression, don't think that you are ready for a full workload yet. You are still in recovery, not completely well yet, and if you rush back too soon and expect to fire on all cylinders, you will only get over-stressed and exhausted, and this will impede a quick recovery. Getting over a depressive illness takes time, and although at this stage you probably want to put every thought of depression behind you, it isn't wise to put yourself under too much pressure to do so. When you feel you are ready for work, go back, but don't immediately take on heavy commitments. Remember, if one of your colleagues took time off work for a serious medical condition such as a heart attack, you would expect him to ease back into the job in his own time. Your bout of depression deserves the same respect.

- Apply the same strategy to your social life. Socialising is supposed to be fun and relaxing, but when you have been depressed and out of the loop for a while, a room full of people may seem daunting, especially as you might be called upon to explain your absence. So for the time being, stick to close friends, and don't attempt large, stressful gatherings where you are expected to be on top form.

- Be open about your health problem. Hiding depressive illness is just reinforcing and perpetuating the mistaken view that it is a condition to be ashamed of, which won't help you now, or indeed others who need access to treatment in the future. At this stage, when you have been isolated inside your depression, you need to feel part of the gang again. People always find out what has been wrong with you anyway, and you want to avoid others being embarrassed or talking behind your back when your confidence is still a little shaky. Now that you can say there is a treatment both to alleviate your depression and help prevent you from getting it in the future, it really is something you should be telling everyone about! Talk to a few of your closer colleagues at work, rather than making a public statement to the whole office. There is probably a high percentage of your friends and work colleagues who have suffered themselves, and they will be delighted that there is a successful natural alternative to antidepressant drugs. You will be surprised at how sympathetic most people will be.

- Mend your fences with your family and friends. Now you are feeling better, it is perhaps time to take a good look at how those in your immediate environment have been affected by your illness. If you have been diagnosed and treated quite quickly, this may not be a problem, but for many, as we have discussed, there can be a long period of dysfunctional depressive behaviour before the symptoms lift. For instance, you might have leaned heavily on one particular friend or family member. They might be exhausted and slightly resentful about the time they have expended covering for you, especially if you have been drinking heavily. Your partner may have had to carry a double burden of keeping the family ticking over, or a work colleague may have been doing some of your job as well as their own. Maybe your children have not fully understood your illness, and need an explanation as to why you haven't been your usual supportive self. Your friends may want reassurance about why you suddenly deserted them. You don't have to apologise for your depression, but it can help to thank the people who have supported you during your difficult time, and appreciate what your illness has meant to them.

- Get your body moving. For weeks, or maybe even months, you have probably been slumped and scrunched up, feeling lethargic and unwilling to exert yourself. You may have been reluctant to face the gym, your Saturday football game, or morning swim, so your body muscles and tissue will have become pretty stagnant. Getting the oxygen flowing through your system and burning off those stress hormones will make you feel so much better and will greatly contribute to your recovery. And any weight you might have put on during your depression will begin to disappear once you become more active again. But don't overdo it and risk injury. Check out the Exercise Tips on the next page.

- Remember that recovery may not be consistent. You may feel better one day, then experience moments of hopelessness the next. This is normal and doesn't mean that your treatment isn't working. These moments will get less frequent, so take heart. It could be a few months before you really feel properly yourself again.

Exercise Tips

- Start small. Just go for a walk. If this feels aimless, then pick a place you need to get to and walk instead of taking some form of transport. Being out in the daylight alone will boost your mood.
- Try to walk quite briskly, stand tall and breathe deeply. This will give you plenty of fresh air and oxygen.
- Or find an exercise you enjoy, perhaps swimming, cycling, jogging, and start by doing it twice a week for at least twenty minutes. There is often a compulsion with people who haven't exercised for a long time to rush in and overdo it. Take your time, or you risk injury, which will not help your mood.
- Think, Move! Move about more during the day. So, for instance, walk to the next bus/Tube stop, take the dog a bit further, use the stairs not the lift, don't take the car for short distances. It is so easy when you are depressed to stay slumped in one place for hours on end.
- If you are getting stiff as you get older, find a ten-minute stretching programme you can do at home, plus a brisk half-hour walk three times a week. Then you can gradually increase as your strength and stamina improve.
- Don't push yourself, this should be pleasure, not punishment.
- Buy a comfortable pair of walking shoes and carry smarter ones in your bag.
- Don't forget to drink lots of water.

STAGE 3. FULL RECOVERY FROM DEPRESSION

There will come a wonderful time when you reach this final stage in the course of your depressive illness. You realise, at last, that you are feeling well again, that you have got yourself back, part of the 'you' that you recognise from before the depression, and it's a great realisation. But depression does change people, and the chances are that you will feel like a different person now you have successfully come through a bout of depression. Most of these changes will be positive, such as feeling stronger for having come through the ordeal, knowing yourself better as a result of confronting your demons, getting a perspective on what matters in your life, and being aware of the love and support that surround you. But there can sometimes be negative fallout from depression that needs to be addressed.

- One of the biggest problems that people who have overcome depression experience is fear of a recurrence. One man explained it this way: 'I feel fine now, but I can still see those little black gremlins lurking on the outskirts of my mind, waiting to come back and torment me again, and it terrifies me.' Once you have experienced depression, the thought of visiting that darkness again can be very worrying. However, Dr Puri's experience with his patients on EPA is that as long as they continue to take the supplement, they can keep further bouts of illness at bay. One of his patients did come off EPA, and his symptoms threatened to return, but after he went back on the high-dose supplement, they disappeared again. So if you have recently recovered from depression, continue taking your EPA supplement and you should avoid a distressing recurrence of your symptoms.

- Another problem you might encounter is loss of confidence in yourself. Depression makes you feel intensely vulnerable and plays games with your mind. During a bout of depression you can begin to question who you are and what purpose your life represents. It can begin to feel as if you don't know yourself. Even when you have recovered, you tend to re-examine what you understand about yourself. No one imagines they could be a depressed person, just as no one believes they will ever be a cancer patient or a diabetic, until it happens to them. Illness is always something that happens to other people. So it is profoundly unnerving to realise that you can be vulnerable in this way, and that you can feel such extreme despair. Facing the world with this new experience and knowledge about yourself, however, can change your perspective on your life. It can mean different priorities and a fresh focus about how you live your life, and is a very positive outcome, but it can take time to feel completely at home with the changed 'you'.
- You might also sense a loss of confidence about yourself in those around you. The stigma of depression is gradually being eroded as the disease is talked of more and there is a new level of understanding about the cause and outcome. But there are still lingering pockets of prejudice, which you might be unfortunate enough to encounter. What should you do if you feel that you are being judged for merely falling victim to a disease? Obviously it depends very much on the situation. For instance, a partner might feel that they have seen a side to you that they never knew existed and that alarmed them. They might worry, like you, that you will have another attack of depression, and they might feel they can no longer rely on you. If this is the case, you can now reassure them by informing them

about the disease and its optimistic prognosis in the light of EPA, and it might also help, as we suggested above, to let them know how the illness affected you. The more people understand about depression, the less they will see the symptoms as personality shortcomings. If you feel those at work have lost confidence in your abilities, and your illness is threatening your job, it is important to reassure your colleagues that you have found a treatment that will help keep you well and free from further episodes. But don't give in to prejudice. You have been ill, you have not developed a personality defect, and when you have fully recovered, you should be able to do your job just as well as you did before you became ill; perhaps, with your new-found self-knowledge, even better.

- Questioning your relationships with friends and family can be one of the knock-on effects of surviving a depressive episode. While those close to you might have been bewildered and worried by your illness, you yourself might also harbour some lingering resentment about their level of support during your depression. This is understandable, but remember that unless they have experienced depression themselves, they can have very little idea of what you were going through, particularly if you were unable to explain and, as a result, you shut them out. You might feel a friend deserted you, but maybe they didn't understand your strange behaviour either. Clearing the air by voicing unspoken resentments is important if you are to get your relationships back on track. You don't need to make a saga out of it, just give everyone involved, including yourself, the chance to have their say.

These are some of the strategies you can employ to cope with any problems you may encounter in the aftermath of your illness. There is also a very positive message to all of you who have just recovered from depression. You have survived! You have been through a taxing time, but you have recovered and now you face the rest of your life with far greater understanding and strength.

Protecting Your Future

As we discussed earlier, depression has many triggers. Lack of EPA is certainly an important biological context, but there are also other psychological and physical triggers. There is no point in dwelling too long on the events or circumstances that set off your depression now that you have recovered, but it makes sense to be aware of what they were and to be conscious of similar situations should they occur in the future. When you have recovered and are feeling strong again, take a background check on what might have triggered your episode by asking these questions:

1. Was there a difficult life event that occurred in the weeks or months prior to my depression?
2. Had I experienced this sort of trauma before, and if so, did it trigger depression that time too?
3. Was I under stress in other areas of my life?
4. Do I compromise my health by not looking after my general physical welfare?
5. Do I have addictive habits such as heavy drinking or drug-taking?
6. Had I been ill?
7. Are there unresolved traumatic events in my childhood, such as persistent neglect or loss of a main carer?
8. Am I someone who suffers from low self-esteem?

Answer honestly, and try to pinpoint which of these triggers might have contributed to your recent depression. There might be more than one. When you have identified the contributory factor or factors, see if there are things about your lifestyle that you can change to avoid these same triggers being a problem in the future.

'Yes' to Questions 1 and 2: your depression is obviously triggered by your reaction to traumatic events. You can't avoid all trauma in your life, or in the lives of people close to you such as your children, but you can be aware that you may be especially vulnerable when faced with these events. When next you experience trauma, such as the loss of someone you love, make sure you don't repress your emotions regarding your loss. Find someone to talk to, either friend, family member or therapist, who can listen to and support you through your bereavement. If you recognise this as a trigger for past depressive episodes too, then you have to be doubly on your guard against sliding into depressive symptoms. And make sure you are fortifying your body systems with an EPA supplement.

'Yes' to Question 3: take a look at all areas of your life. Were you pushing yourself too hard and being unrealistic in your goals? Were you having relationship difficulties? Had you recently been unhappy in your job? Are you someone who finds it hard to wind down? This is the time to make some changes in your stress levels and learn how to relax. Perhaps you need to take up yoga or t'ai chi, or learn meditation. Perhaps you need to spend more time at home and less at work. Perhaps you can get your family to help out more with the household chores and give you some free time. But you should also consider removing things from your life that don't work for you, such as a job you hate or a relationship that makes you unhappy.

'Yes' to Question 4: it might be time to start a regular exercise programme and stop eating all those ready meals and junk food. Don't become obsessive about your diet, just gradually replace the junk with more fruit, vegetables and healthy oils.

'Yes' to Question 5: give them up! Get help if necessary. It won't be easy, but it isn't easy being depressed either.

'Yes' to Question 6: watch out for illnesses that are associated with depression. We list them in Chapter 3.

'Yes' to Questions 7 and 8: you might consider therapy. Unresolved issues have a nasty habit of coming back to haunt you, and clearly your depression might be a result of these ghosts. It may be difficult at first, but a good therapist will only allow you to confront difficult issues when you are ready.

Keep Informed about Your Health

One of the greatest problems we face in recognising, treating and avoiding any disease, most particularly depression, is ignorance. Many of us are just not educated about our health. At school we may study frogs and dog-fish in biology, with a passing glance at the human reproductive tract, and that is the sum total of our knowledge of human anatomy and physiology. So we are completely ignorant about how our bodies actually work. Then if we fall ill, we entrust ourselves blindly to the overworked hands of our GP, who will barely have time to diagnose and prescribe, let alone explain the details of our problem and its treatment.

Nowadays we need not be so ignorant. The Internet is an easily accessible tool to help us acquire basic information, and from there we can access organisations, support groups, specialist practitioners, drug and nutritional advances and further reading to enhance that knowledge. And we can become better informed as a way of preventing illness, not just as a means of finding the most up-to-date treatment available. Check out the Internet sources at the back of the book, and find out the latest research into depression and any other medical condition you might be suffering from, or for the latest general health news. By doing this you will be giving yourself the best chance of a healthy future.

Natural Therapies to Aid Your Recovery

There are various natural therapies, such as acupuncture, shiatsu massage and aromatherapy, that can help and support you while you are being treated for, and during your recovery from, depression. Therapies that stimulate and release the flow of energy through the body are beneficial for many physical and emotional problems, including pain relief, weight loss, quitting smoking and insomnia. These therapies are also a great pick-me-up for when you are worn out by depression, and can be useful in conjunction with EPA supplementation as an integrated approach to help speed your recovery.

If you want to find a fully qualified practitioner in these therapies, look at the back of the book for professional associations, or check out your local health centre or library.

ACUPUNCTURE

An ancient technique, this is an aspect of traditional Chinese medicine (TCM) that is one of the most popular complementary therapies in the West, and one in which even the medical profession have faith, with some doctors now including acupuncture in an integrated approach to healing.

And there have been numerous research studies which back up the efficacy of this treatment system.

It works by stimulating points, known as acupoints, along the meridians, or energy channels that run through the body. This is done by inserting fine acupuncture needles. When the acupoints are stimulated in this way, the energy paths are cleared and your body energy is unblocked and balanced. The needles are very fine, and most people either are not aware of them being inserted, or feel a mild discomfort. You may feel tired or emotional after a treatment, and often the symptoms get worse before they get better and the body rebalances. But you should feel more clear-headed, less sluggish, and your sleep and digestion should improve. You should only consider a fully qualified practitioner.

MASSAGE

A technique for releasing muscle tension, it is also a form of healing through human touch. Particularly if you are recovering from depression and feeling anxious, run-down and low in energy, a massage can bring you a great sense of relaxation and wellbeing. It should be a regular part of your health routine. When the skin and soft tissue of the body are stimulated by touch during massage, the flow of oxygen round the body is improved, the lymph glands are stimulated to eliminate toxins such as stress hormones, the muscles are relaxed and endorphins — good-mood chemicals — are released.

There are many different massage techniques, but a good one to help with your recovery from depression is shiatsu, which is a full-body holistic massage. Shiatsu is based on the same principles as acupuncture, except the practitioner uses their thumbs, fingers, elbows and occasionally knees instead of needles to stimulate the acupoints along the meridian lines. It originated in Japan, but it has roots in traditional Chinese medicine. The few seconds when an acupoint is being pressed can be quite uncomfortable, but a skilled therapist will be sensitive to your tolerance. Shiatsu is very effective in helping depression, fatigue, insomnia, migraine and stress-related conditions. For the best results you will probably need to see the practitioner a number of times, and regularly if possible, so choose someone you feel completely comfortable with and make sure they are fully qualified.

AROMATHERAPY

This adds the healing properties of essential oils to the benefits of massage. We have talked about healthy oils in your diet, and the theory behind aromatherapy is that essential oils from plants can also be used on a psychological and physiological level to heal when topically applied rather than ingested. Aromatherapy is commonly used to reduce stress and tension, to balance body energy, support the immune system, and to bring about a sense of calm and wellbeing.

As well as inhaling essential oils during massage, you can also benefit from them in a scented bath, through a vaporiser or on a pillow or handkerchief. So treat yourself to a warm bath or a massage with some sweet orange, which refreshes the mind, encourages a positive outlook, and relieves tension and stress. Or try clary sage, which is effective in lifting your mood and reducing anxiety and nervous tension (not advised during pregnancy or with alcohol). Or rosewood, which relieves stress and tension. These oils, unlike the EFA-rich oils we have mentioned, are not safe to take internally as they are extremely concentrated and would prove toxic.

Spiritual Disciplines to Aid Your Recovery

When you are fully on the path to recovery, it might be worth considering taking up a technique, such as yoga, t'ai chi or meditation, which offers ways in which you can strengthen your body and relax your mind, helping to reduce the stress in your life and so avoid another bout of depressive illness.

YOGA

Yoga is an ancient Eastern philosophy and system of movement which was devised to address all aspects of mind and body to encourage spiritual enlightenment. It tones, strengthens and mobilises your body, and is a gentle way to get your system moving after the stagnation of depression. Regular practice also calms the mind and greatly enhances spiritual wellbeing. It is strongly recommended as an antidote to stress.

The most commonly practised yoga in the West is hatha yoga, which uses postural movements called *asanas*, breath-work called *pranayama*, and meditation, called *dyana*. Learn from a qualified teacher at a yoga centre at first; don't struggle with a book or videotape. Yoga is not competitive, and you can go at your own pace.

T'AI CHI

This is one of the numerous Chinese movement systems going back thousands of years. It is a martial art and also a mind, body, spirit exercise system. The aim, as with yoga, is to make the body stronger and more flexible and at the same time free the energy pathways through the body, so that your body energy flows more freely. T'ai chi is a gentle, graceful discipline which involves a series of poses linked with fluid movements, and has been termed a 'moving meditation'. It is concerned with relaxation, balance and grounding the body. It is excellent for dealing with stress and anxiety, and would be ideal if you are just coming out of a bout of depression for getting your body moving without strain. Find a qualified teacher, as the system involves breathwork and meditation as well as a large number of different postures.

MEDITATION

Everyone can benefit from the practice, not just New Age followers, and studies have shown that regular meditation reduces stress and helps alleviate depression. It also encourages self-awareness, calms your mind and can even lower your blood pressure, so it is the perfect discipline if you want to control your levels of stress and increase your confidence after a depressive illness.

Meditation works by changing the level of brain activity from the normal alert, waking state, characterised by beta waves, to the slower, more meditative levels characterised by alpha, theta and the lowest level of brain activity, delta. By slowing your mind, but still being aware, you are able to access the vast potential of your mind, and to become detached from petty thoughts and worries. This detachment allows a perspective on yourself and your life which, over time, can help you become calm and mentally strong. This is a form of meditation known as Vipissana developed by the Tibetan Buddhists. The technique is wonderfully simple.

- First you should understand that there is no success or failure in any meditation, just practice. Don't judge your performance, because the first few times will probably seem useless and chaotic if you do.

- Dedicate fifteen minutes of your time. It helps to get into a routine and meditate at the same time every day, perhaps in the morning before the day begins.
- Find a quiet place with no phones, people or noise.
- Sit comfortably on a chair, or cross-legged on the floor if you prefer. Make sure you are warm enough.
- Sit straight by imagining you have a string pulling you upwards from the centre of your crown.
- Relax your muscles both internally and externally.
- Breathing through your nose, in and out, without strain or effort, close your eyes and concentrate on your breath in, and your breath out. Feel the air as it enters your body, feel it gently leaving.

That is it. Do this for ten minutes to start with, then build to twenty as it begins to come more naturally. At first you will despair as your thoughts crowd in and distract you, but the more you fight them, the more they will interrupt you. So with each thought that comes, acknowledge it briefly as if it were a performer on a stage, then say goodbye as you watch it drift across the stage and disappear. Return to your breathing. Do this with every intrusive thought, and after a while you will enjoy a sense of calm. When your ten minutes are up, open your eyes and take a couple of deep breaths. You will find yourself refreshed. As you get more experienced, you will be able to access more and more of your inner self, and in moments of stress or panic in the outside world you will know a place where you can be still.

All these therapies require commitment. You won't feel much benefit from a single session, or sporadic attendance at a class. So make sure you are enjoying your choice and not just doing it because you feel you ought to. If you stick with a partic-ular discipline you will soon find it becomes a regular part of your life you would not be without, and is an excellent way to improve and maintain your spiritual and mental wellbeing.

What EPA Means for All Depression Sufferers

Supplementing with EPA is clearly beneficial to most of us, even if we are not ill. But, as we have seen from Dr Puri's research, it has particular significance for the depression sufferer. The reason for writing this book has been to let all of you who are associated with this difficult disease know about Dr Puri's breakthrough, so that you can begin to reap the benefits of his work and treat your depression with a substance that is both natural and side-effect-free. But it is also to be hoped that his natural treatment option will change the way we view depression.

Once everyone knows that the disease can be treated successfully with a natural substance that does not carry the worry of strong drugs and side effects and that protects you from future episodes of depression, perhaps many more people will come forward to ask for help in treating their depressive symptoms. The more people ask for help, the less hidden and stigmatised the disease will become. Depression could then become an illness like any of the hundreds of other easily treatable conditions from which we occasionally suffer and then recover. If this happens, then Dr Puri and his colleagues will have made a scientific breakthrough that could signifi-cantly reduce the economic, emotional and social cost of an illness that now poses such a burgeoning health threat world-wide. In fact, there has probably never been a better time for you to be depressed.

Here is a round-up of points for you to remember about the general benefits to you of natural EPA, and how the discovery of EPA as an antidepressant has changed our understanding of the causes of depression and how it can be treated.

- EPA is the first successful, scientifically tested, natural, side-effect-free treatment for depression.
- You need no longer worry about the unpleasant side effects of antidepressants.
- EPA can be taken in conjunction with other medication.
- Aside from treating depression, EPA has many other health benefits.
- Everyone can take EPA safely, with the exception of those already on anticoagulant medication.
- EPA can be taken to help prevent depressive illness as well as treat it.
- EPA can be taken as a general health supplement.
- Diet and lifestyle have a serious impact on our health.
- Learning about health is a way of protecting against disease.
- Attitudes to depression are changing slowly. Soon, we hope, there will be no stigma attached to being depressed.
- Surviving depression is a tough journey, but those who survive can be strengthened by their experience.

Depression is a Journey

Any illness will take its toll, but depression, because it affects us emotionally as well as physically, takes us on a difficult journey, which begins when we first experience the distressing darkness of low mood and loss of pleasure, and ends when we emerge back into the sunlight with our feelings alive and intact. You will probably feel that you are unfortunate to have suffered, or be suffering, from depression. As we have discussed, it is a taxing and debilitating disease. But try looking at it this way instead. Many of us go through life without having to question who we are or where we are going. We worry about the mortgage and the children, we focus on our jobs, but we aren't called upon to do much soul-searching.

If you have been depressed, however, you will know what it is like to be turned inwards, to be forced to shut out the practicalities of life and focus only on your feelings and anxieties. It is certainly uncomfortable and distressing while it is happening, but in many cases depression helps turn the sufferer into a more self-aware, rounded and sensitive person. We come face to face with our demons, and survive, and that, surely, is a cause for celebration. We wish you well on your journey, and hope that you will recover quickly and enjoy a future free from depressive illness.

Glossary

Adrenaline: a hormone secreted by the adrenal glands in response to stress.

Alpha-linolenic acid (ALA): this is the 'parent' fatty acid at the beginning of the omega-3 metabolic pathway.

Amino acids: chemical compounds in the body that help build proteins.

Anticoagulant: a drug or supplement that lengthens the time it takes for the blood to clot, thus preventing unwanted blood clots in veins and arteries in the body.

Anti-inflammatory: a drug or supplement that reduces inflammation in body tissues.

Arachidonic acid (AA): an omega-6 EFA metabolised from GLA.

Beta-blockers: drugs that lower blood pressure by slowing the heart rate or improving blood flow in the arteries by preventing the arteries from contracting.

Bipolar disorder (manic depression): where a person experiences episodes of both mania and depression.

Clinical depression: depression triggered by a biochemical imbalance, such as low levels of EFAs.

Cognitive therapy: psychotherapy that helps correct distorted thought patterns and a low self-image by teaching techniques that offer a more realistic approach to life.

Computed tomography (CT): an X-ray scan used to take images of the brain and body.

Cortisol: a steroid hormone produced in the adrenal glands and released during stress.

Docosahexaenoic acid (DHA): an omega-3 EFA metabolised from EPA important in eye and brain health.

Dopamine: a neurotransmitter that affects the pleasure centres of the brain and is involved with control of body movement.

Double-blind trial: this means that the doctor treating the patient does not know who is taking the placebo and who is taking the real substance being tested. This is to avoid the patient being subconsciously influenced by the doctor's attitudes or beliefs.

Eicosapentaenoic acid (EPA): this nutrient is an essential fatty acid primarily found in fish oil.

Endocrine system: a system that consists of a number of hormone-secreting organs such as the thyroid and adrenal glands.

Essential fatty acids (EFAs): a fatty acid is one of the 'building blocks' of a fat molecule. They do not exist in the body and have to be obtained from food.

Ethyl-EPA: the pure ethyl form of EPA which does not contain any other EFAs.

Evening primrose oil (EPO): oil from the seeds of the evening primrose plant that contains a pure form of GLA.

Gamma linolenic acid (GLA): an omega-6 EFA that plays many roles in your body's health, including maintaining healthy cells and helping produce prostaglandins.

Glial cells: these cells are responsible for supporting neurons by feeding them vital nutrients and providing the best biochemical environment for the nerve cells in the brain.

Grey matter: the brain's cerebral cortex which is filled with millions of neurons and glial cells.

Haemoglobin: the iron-containing protein that fills red blood cells.

Highly unsaturated fatty acid (HUFA): these fatty acids are made up of very fluid carbon chains. There are two different kinds, the omega-3 type and the omega-6 type.

Hormones: chemical substances produced by the endocrine and other glands in the body which influence mood and trigger bodily functions.

Hydrogenated fat: a process where healthy unsaturated oils are turned into unhealthy saturated fats.

Hyperkinetic: hyperactive.

Hypothalamus: an area of the brain that releases hormones, which in turn trigger the pituitary gland to release more hormones, which in turn affect various glands in the body.

Hypothyroidism: underactivity of the thyroid gland, symptoms of which can mimic depression.

Linoleic acid (LA): this is the 'parent' fatty acid at the beginning of the omega-6 metabolic pathway

Lipids: compounds in the body that contain fatty acids.

Magnetic resonance imaging (MRI): a brain scanning technique using powerful magnets to create images which measure the size of the brain ventricles and brain activity.

Mastalgia: breast pain brought on by an imbalance of the sex hormones oestrogen and progesterone.

Metabolise: to break down or build up biochemical substances in the body to effect processes such as energy production.

Monoamine oxidase inhibitor (MAOI): older form of antidepressant which raises neurotransmitter levels in the brain.

Neuron: a nerve cell. Neurons transmit electrical impulses across the brain to send messages to the rest of the body.

Neurotransmitters: chemicals in the brain which help electrical impulses, or messages, jump across the gap between one neuron and another.

Noradrenaline: a neurotransmitter and a chemical that is associated with physical and mental excitement. It is also involved, like serotonin, in mood regulation.

Oestrogens: a group of sex hormones secreted mainly by the ovaries.

Omega-3 fatty acids: a type of fatty acid family including ALA, EPA and DHA.

Omega-6 fatty acids: a type of fatty acid family including LA, GLA and AA.

Phospholipids: complex fat molecules which are found in every cell in the body, and which form a layer to protect and enhance the connectivity of the brain messages.

Pineal gland: secretes the hormone melatonin, the hormone that helps us sleep.

Placebo: an inactive substance that is made up to look like an active drug and used in drug trials.

Polyunsaturated fatty acid (PUFA): an unsaturated fatty acid with more than one link between the carbon atoms in its structure. All EFAs are PUFAs.

Prophylactic: a drug, technique or action used to prevent or protect against disease.

Prostaglandins: hormone-like substances made in the phospholipid layer in the cell membrane, which regulate many bodily functions.

Protein: a molecule that is made up of a number of amino acids. Proteins are vital for all life processes.

Psychosis: a mental response that can include hallucinations or delusions, and implies losing contact with reality.

Randomised: this term is the process of allocation in a drug trial. Patients are either allocated the substance being tested, or a placebo, in an entirely random way.

Reactive depression: depression triggered by external events, such as bereavement.

Saturated fat: fat that is solid at room temperature, particularly dairy products such as butter, cheese and fat on red meat.

Serotonin: a neurotransmitter, low levels of which are linked to depression.

SSRI (Serotonin Re-uptake Inhibitor): the most popular type of antidepressant drug currently in use, which raises levels of serotonin in the brain.

Synapse: the tiny gap between the neurons in the brain.

Trans fats: over-processed fats that prevent the healthy metabolising of EFAs in the body.

Tricyclic: older form of antidepressant drug which raises neurotransmitter levels in the brain.

Unsaturated fat: unrefined vegetable oils, such as flax, olive and walnut.

Ventricles: chambers either in the brain or the heart.

Further Resources

Relevant Internet Sites

The British National Formulary (BNF): up-to-date information on the side effects of currently available antidepressants. Look for current edition, BNF 47, on publisher's websites.
www.pharmpress.com and *www.bmjbookshop.com*

Equazen: a good site for latest research and information about fatty acids and brain disorders such as depression, dyslexia and ADHD. It also has information about eye q. Product ordering phone line: 44 (0) 0870 2415621.
www.equazen.com

Genulex Cream: product ordering phone line: 44 (0) 1223 514606.
www.avatoninternational.com

Healthcastle.com: general information about health and nutritional issues, including information about trans fats.
www.healthcastle.com

The Marine Conservation Society: details about how to buy fish from sustainable sources.
www.mcsuk.org

Morepa: *www.mor-epa.com*

Maxepa: type in Maxepa to search engine to find the various supplement suppliers.

PSYweb: a comprehensive American site offering on-line information about mental illness and psychiatric medications.
www.psyweb.com

PubMed: summaries of all the major medical and scientific research that has been published in leading international journals, free of charge.
www.ncbi.nim.nih.gov/PubMed
Another site that enables you to discover how much trans fats are present in different foods is at:
Napa.ntdt.udel.edu/trans/default.html

VegEPA: product ordering phone line: 44 (0) 1223 514606.
www.vegepa.com

Recommended Books

Blake Tracy, Dr Ann, *Prozac: Panacea or Pandora?*, Cassia Publications (1994)

Bowlby, John, *Attachment and Loss*, Penguin (1981)

Further Resources

Breggin, Dr Peter R., *The Antidepressant Fact Book: What Your Doctor Won't Tell You about Prozac, Zoloft, Paxil, Celaxa, and Luvox,* Perseus Books (2001)

Breggin, Dr Peter R., and Cohen, Dr David, *Your Drug May Be Your Problem: How and Why to Stop Taking Psychiatric Medications,* Perseus Books (2001)

DePaulo, Dr J. Raymond, Jr, *Understanding Depression,* John Wiley (2002)

Earle, Liz, *New Vital Oils,* Vermilion (2002)

Healy, David, *The Antidepressant Era,* Harvard University Press (1997)

Horrobin, Professor David, *The Madness of Adam and Eve,* Corgi (2002)

Kramer, Dr Peter D., *Listening to Prozac,* Penguin (revised edition 1997)

Rowe, Dorothy, *Depression,* Routledge (1996)

Smith, Dr Tony (medical editor), *British Medical Association Complete Family Health Guide,* Dorling Kindersley (2000)

Wolpert, Lewis, *Malignant Sadness,* Faber and Faber (1999)

Useful Organisations

Action on Smoking and Health (ASH)
102 Clifton Street
London EC2A 4HW
Tel: 020 7739 5902
Helpline: 0800 002200
www.ash.org.uk

Alcoholics Anonymous
Box 1, Stonebow House
York YO1 7NJ
Tel: 01904 644026
Helpline: 0207 833 0022
www.alcoholics-anonymous.org.uk

Association for Postnatal Illness
25 Jerdan Place
London SW6 1BE
Tel: 020 7386 0868
www.apni.org

British Acupuncture Council
63 Jeddo Road
London W12 9HQ
020 8735 0400
www.acupuncture.org.uk

British Association of Psychotherapists
37 Mapesbury Road
London NW2 4HJ
Tel: 020 8452 9823
www.bap-psychotherapy.org

Further Resources

The British Massage Therapy Council
78 Meadow Street
Preston
Lancashire PR1 1TS
Tel: 01772 881063
www.jolanta.co.uk

Cruse Bereavement Care
126 Sheen Road
Richmond
Surrey TW9 1UR
Tel: 020 8940 4818
www.crusebereavementcare.org.uk

Depression Alliance
35 Westminster Bridge Road
London SE1 7JB
Tel: 020 7633 9929
www.depressionalliance.org.uk

Institute of Complementary Medicine
PO Box 194
London SE16 7QZ
Tel: 020 7237 5165
www.icmedicine.co.uk

The International Society of Professional Aromatherapists
82 Ashby Road
Hinckley
Leicestershire LE10 1SN
Tel: 01455 637987
www.the-ispa.org

MIND (National Association for Mental Health)
15–19 Broadway
London E15 4QB
Mindinfoline: 020 8522 1728
Outside London: 0345 660163
www.mind.org.uk

Narcotics Anonymous
PO Box 417
London SW10 0RP
Tel: 020 7351 6794
www.ukna.org

SADA (Seasonal Affective Disorder Association)
PO Box 989
Steyning
West Sussex BN44 3HG
Tel: 01903 814942
www.sada.org.uk

The Samaritans
10 The Grove
Slough SL1 1QP
Tel: 01753 2165000
Helpline: 0345 909090
www.samaritans.org.uk

School of T'ai Chi Chuan
Centre for Healing
5 Tavistock Place
London WC1H 9SN
Tel: 020 8444 6445
www.chinatown-online.co.uk

Sivananda Yoga Vedanta Centre
51 Felsham Road
London SW15 1AZ
Tel: 020 8780 0160
www.sivananda.org

Index

AA *see* arachidonic acid
Action for Smoking and
    Health (ASH) 182
acupuncture 198, 223–4
Adapin 134
Addenbrooke's Hospital,
    Cambridge v, vi
addiction 69–71, 211
Addison's disease 7–8, 34
ADHD *see* attention deficit
    disorder
adrenal gland 72, 90
adrenal hormones 34
adrenaline (epinephrine) 84,
    90, 124
    high adrenaline caused by
    stress 176–9
ageing 176
    and EFAs 183–4
agitation 38
agoraphobia 27
Aherne, Caroline 46
AIDS 4
ALA *see* alpha-linolenic acid
alcohol consumption 4, 28,

30, 43, 46, 49, 50, 52, 66,
    69–71, 73, 83, 100, 103,
    161, 176, 178, 186, 187,
    208, 211, 220
    and EFAs 179–81, 184
Alcoholics Anonymous 211
Alison (a patient) 193–5
Allegron 134
allergy 102, 141, 153
almonds and almond oil
    (Prunus amygdalus) 171
alpha-linolenic acid (ALA) 93,
    94, 96–7, 162, 163
    sources of 95, 169
    see also omega-3
Alzheimer's disease 105
amantadine 74
ambition, lack of 58
American Psychiatric
    Association (APA) 30, 31
amino acids 61
amitriptyline (Triptafen; Elavil;
    Endep) 134
amoxapine (Asendis; Asendin)
    134

amphetamine ('speed') 136
amygdala 91
anaemia 7, 32, 32, 33
Anafranil 134
anger 48, 63
Anthony (a patient) 7–12, 88,
    91–2, 98, 104–9, 108
antibiotics 13
    sulphonamide 74
anticoagulants 145, 146, 153,
    187, 189, 230
anticonvulsants 74
antidepressants 53, 150
    and drug companies 84
    EPA as a supplementary
    treatment 15, 17, 116, 145,
    146, 152
    not taken properly 21, 116,
    118–19
    problems with your doctor's
    choice of 117–20
    and recurrence of depres-
    sion 120, 121–2, 139
    side effects v, vi, 1, 5, 6, 15,
    20, 98, 110, 112, 113, 116,
    118–19, 129–36, 138, 139,
    144, 146, 151
    statistics of current use 123
    suddenly discontinuing a
    course 15, 18, 21, 117,
    118–19, 137, 138
    think twice before taking
    138–9
antipsychotic drugs 39, 53, 74,
    194
antiviral drugs 74
anxiety 27, 33, 36, 48, 72, 74,
    140
APA see American Psychiatric
    Association
apes, humans and 76–7
appetite 8, 11, 27, 34
arachidonic acid (AA) 95, 96,
97, 158
aromatherapy 225
arthritis 102, 155, 164, 185,
    196–8
Asendin 134
Asendis 134
asthma 74, 102, 155
attention deficit disorder
    (ADHD) 155, 202–3, 205
auditory hallucination 29, 38
Aventyl 134
axons 89

'baby blues' 35–6
bacterial infections 74
Beck, Aaron 142
behavioural therapy 142
Belmaker, Professor Robert
    99
benefits of EPA for everyone
    186–99, 230
    attention deficit disorder
    202–3
    better antenatal and post-
    natal health for mother and
    baby 195–6
    better vision 192
    chronic fatigue syndrome
    199–201
    diabetes mellitus complica-
    tions 203–4
    a healthier heart 187–8, 204
    taking anticoagulants 189
    healthy bones and joints
    196–8, 204
    healthy hormone balance
    192–3
    healthy skin and hair
    190–95, 204
    other cardiovascular condi-
    tions 189–90
    schizophrenia 199
benzodiazepines 74

bereavement 24
bereavement counsellor 66
beta–blockers 43, 74
biological factors 41, 55–6, 60–62, 63, 85
  body chemicals 61
  genes 61–2
bipolar disorder (manic depression) 14, 23, 36–7, 53, 91
  treatment 37, 117
bizarre thought patterns 38
blackcurrant seed oil (Ribes nigrum) 172
blood clotting 166
blood pressure 6, 43, 74, 166, 188
borage oil (Borago officinalis) Starflower 172
brain
  brain function improved by EPA vii, viii, 1, 12
  development 56, 78, 79, 80, 196
  how fat reaches the brain 92–3
  how fatty acids affect the brain 93–4
  how it works 87–90
    glial cells 89
    grey matter (cerebral cortex) 88
    neurons 89
    neurotransmitters 89–90
  image registration 108
  levels of EPA in 55–6, 75, 97
  levels of neurotransmitters 5
  and meditation 227
  the parts implicated in depression 90–92
  a pregnant woman's brain 109
  reduced level of activity 88, 111
  regeneration of cells 12, 105, 106, 108, 110, 111
  size 76, 77, 80, 105, 106
  starved of EFAs 46, 61
  understanding the effects of EPA on 104–6
  the well–nourished brain 80, 100, 111, 146, 161
brain chemicals 60
brain imaging techniques 88, 91
brain scans 15
  and pregnant women 109
  to observe the effects of EPA 10, 11–12, 105–6
brain ventricles 11–12, 105, 109
breast pain, monthly cyclical 102
breast-feeding 196, 205
breathing 178

caffeine vii
cancer 3, 4, 20, 32, 52, 155
carbamazepine 37, 74, 117
carbohydrates 92
  craving 35
carcinogens 182
cardiac arrhythmia 188
CAT see cognitive analytic therapy
CBT see cognitive behavioural therapy
Celexa 130
cerebral cortex (grey matter) 12, 88, 91, 100, 105, 106, 128
CFS see chronic fatigue syndrome
change
  coping with 68–9
  unwelcome 62
chemical imbalance 34, 60, 61
childbirth, hormone changes after 34

Index

children
  depression 51, 52
  and divorce 67
  leaving home 67
chimpanzees 76
chloral hydrate 74
chocolate vii
cholesterol 92, 93, 170, 171
cholorpromazine 39
chronic depressive illness 25
chronic fatigue syndrome
  (CFS) 32
  treatment with EPA vii,
  145, 199–201
Churchill, Sir Winston 46
Cipramil 130
citalopram (Cipramil; Celexa)
  130
clomipramine (Anafranil) 134
clonidine 74
cod 163
cod liver oil 197
coffee vii, 178
cognitive analytic therapy
  (CAT) 113, 140, 142–4,
  147, 151–2
cognitive behavioural therapy
  (CBT) 142
cognitive psychologists 58,
  59
'cognitive triad' 58
cold, sensitivity to 33
colds 102
complex lipids 93
concentration 8, 26, 30, 36, 40,
  48, 91, 114, 199
confidence 11, 144
convulsions 131, 134
Cornell University 46
corticosteroids 34, 74
cortisol 72, 90
coughs 102
crying 66

Cushing's syndrome 72
cyclosporin 141

dairy products 73
Darwin, Charles 61
death of someone close to you
  62–5, 99
decision-making 26
deep vein thrombosis (DVT)
  190
delusions 29, 31, 32, 37, 38
dementia 11, 43, 105, 108
dendrites 89
depression
  are you depressed? 47–9
  avoiding recurrence 153–4
  biological factors 4–5, 55–6,
  60–62, 63, 85
  British statistics 20–21
  current treatments options
  15
  defining 22–3
  diagnosis see diagnosis
  different from a low mood
  2, 23–4
  EFA levels linked to 81–2
  genetic component 15,
  44–5, 53
  as an illness 2–3, 52, 86
  no-one immune 46–7, 53
  older people at risk 43, 53
  other natural treatments for
  139–44
  physical factors 71–5, 85
  psychological factors 15, 41,
  55, 56–9, 63, 85
  reaches epidemic proportions 3–4
  recovery see recovery from
  depression
  research 4–6, 84–5
  seen as an inherent weakness
  3, 14

and social deprivation 46–7, 53
social factors 62–71, 85
symptoms *see* symptoms of depression
understanding 14–15
untreated 39–40
who is affected and why 15
in women 15, 41–2, 53
see also bipolar disorder; mild depression; moderate depression; postnatal depression; reactive depression; resistant depression; seasonal affective disorder (SAD); severe depression
Depression Alliance 42
despair 2, 24–5, 53
despondency 36
Desyrel 133
DGLA *see* dihomo-gamma linolenic acid
DHA *see* docosahexaenoic acid
diabetes mellitus 203–4
diagnosis
mild depression 31
moderate depression 31
physical changes 29–30
problems with 32
severe depression 32
diagnostic classification 30–31
Diagnostic and Statistical Manual of Mental Disorders (DSM) (current edition DSM-IV-TR) 30, 44
diet vii, 86, 230
EPA levels vii, 41, 75, 149
high levels of EFAs 63
and optimum health 15
poor 33, 46, 63, 73
the problem with the modern diet 155–7
dieting 104

digoxin 141
dihomo-gamma linolenic acid (DGLA) 95, 96
divorce 4, 62, 64, 67, 186
DNA (deoxyribonucleic acid) 76
identical twins 44
docosahexaenoic acid (DHA) 94–7, 158, 162, 192, 197, 198
doctors
problems with your doctor's choice of antidepressants 117–20, 150–51
visiting your doctor 114–17
dopamine 72, 84, 90, 100, 111, 124, 140
double-blind trials 10, 98, 99, 203
doxepin (Sinequan; Adapin; Zonalon) 134
drinking *see* alcohol consumption
drug companies 5–6, 13, 84, 85, 118, 125, 127, 139
drugs
drug use 4, 8, 28, 30, 43, 46, 63, 66, 69, 70, 131, 208, 211, 220
prescription 74–5
Dutonin 133

E1 prostaglandin 102, 172
eating patterns 50
economic independence 67
economic migration 4, 66–7
'economy class syndrome' 145, 190
eczema 102, 174
Edronax 132
Edwards, Rhian 83
EFAs *see* essential fatty acids
Efexor/Effexor 131

Index

Elavil 134
Eli Lilly (drug company) 125
Ellis, Albert 142
employment
  after recovery 213
  job insecurity 4
  low-paid 45
  redundancy 62
  and untreated depression 40
Endep 134
endocrine system 72
EPA (eicosapentaenoic acid)
  advantages of taking 144–6
  and anticoagulants 145
  antidepressant action in
  schizophrenia vi–vii, 6,
  9–10, vi–vii, 6, 9–10, 97
  benefits for everyone see
  benefits of EPA for
  everyone
  and brain function vii, viii,
  1, 12, 75, 92–3, 100, 105–6,
  110, 111
  breakthrough research
  studies 98–8
  choice of EPA and not
  another HUFA 96–8
  derivation 94
  a derivative of EFAs 9, 16,
  92
  the EPA Theory 75–85
    Aquatic Dweller 78–9
    a diet rich in EFAs
    80–81
    EFA levels linked to
    depression 81–2
    EFAs are pinpointed
    79–80
    genesis of the idea 76–7
    opposition in the
    medical community 84–5
    Savannah Dweller 77–8
    testing for EFAs 82–4

getting treatment 16–17
a HUFA 93
and Huntington's chorea
vii, 107–11
levels of 55–6, 61, 75, 76,
86, 97
mood-stabilising properties
37
opposition to the theory
12–13
and the phospholipid bilayer
97
proof of its success as a
depression treatment 91–2
and St John's wort 142
and schizophrenia vi–vii, 6,
9–10, 97, 107–8, 110, 111
side-effect-free vii, 1, 10,
53, 98, 142, 145, 146, 151
sources of 95
stem cells stimulated 12, 106
strong scientific basis for its
success 120, 146
supplementation see supplementing with EPA
tackles the root biochemical
cause of depression 128
understanding the effects of
EPA on the brain 104–6
why EPA is the safer, more
reliable option over antidepressants 120–29
  the EPA theory versus
  the monoamine theory
  120, 122–8
  the reliability of EPA
  over antidepressants
  120–21, 128–9
  tackling the recurrence
  of depression with EPA
  120, 121–2, 145
epithelium 192
essential amino acids 61

essential fatty acids (EFAs) vi, viii, 9
  ageing and 183–4
  alcohol consumption and 179–81
  a brain starved of 46, 61
  definition 92
  difficult for the body to make its own EFAs 16
  EPA a derivative of 9, 16, 92
  habits that strip the body of EFAs 103–4
  how they are linked to depression 99–101
  levels in mood disorders 80
  levels in multiple sclerosis 73
  low intake 100
  maintaining high level in diet 101
  and saturated fat 38, 97, 100
  smoking and 181–3
  source of 9, 92
  symptoms of low levels 101–2, 128
  testing for 82–4
  the well-nourished brain 80, 146
  see also under supplementing with EPA
ethyl-EPA 10, 11
evening primrose oil (Oenothera biennis) 172, 191, 197
excitability 140
exercise 178, 216
exhaustion 24, 48, 99
extra virgin olive oil (Olea europea) 170, 184
eye contact 7, 11, 30
eye damage 6
eye q TM 149

facial changes 30
family 4
family and friends
  helping them to get treatment 51–2
  irritation at 48
  mending fences with 214–15
  questioning relationships with 219
  recognising the problem 50
  support by 18
  understanding the problem 50–51
fast food 175
fatigue 35, 36, 199, 225
fats 92
  healthy 159
  not all fats are bad 157–8
  unhealthy 158
fatty acids
  definition 92
  how they affect the brain 93–4
  see also essential fatty acids
Faverin 130
fish consumption, and post-natal depression 81–2, 81
fish oils, oily fish 1, 6, 9, 81, 97, 145, 149, 162, 163–6, 167, 184, 187, 188, 188, 197, 198
flax oil (linseed) (Linum usitatissumum) 168–9, 172, 184
fluid retention 33, 166
fluoxetine see Prozac
fluvoxamine (Faverin; Luvox) 130
folic acid 73
food intolerance 73
Food Standards Agency UK 163–4, 165

Index

foods *see under* supplementing
   with EPA
fried food 175
friends *see* family and friends
frontal cortex 91

gamma-linolenic acid (GLA)
   158, 172, 191, 197
gender issue 15
genes 60, 61–2
genetic component 15, 44–5,
   53
Genulex cream 198
GLA *see* gamma-linolenic acid
glial cells 88, 89, 105
glycerol 92, 93
goitre 33–4
gorillas 76
grey matter *see* cerebral cortex
grief 57, 62, 63, 65, 66
guilt 25, 32, 40

haddock 163
hair
   dry 102
   EPA of benefit to health of
      vii, 145, 191–2, 204
   weak 173–4
hallucinations 29, 31, 32, 37,
   38, 39
   auditory 29
   olfactory 29
Hammersmith Hospital 109,
   200
happiness 24
Hardy, Professor Alister 78
hay fever 102
headaches 199
Healy, Dr David vi
heart attack 188, 204
heart disease 20, 52, 153, 155,
   164, 185
   the biggest problem in the

Western world 4
   depressed men and 21
   treatment with EPA vii, 145
Helen (a patient) 201
helicobacter-pylori organism
   12–13
helplessness 57
Hemingway, Ernest 46
herring 163
Hibbeln, Dr Joseph R. 81, 82
'highly' unsaturated fatty acids
   (HUFA) 93, 94, 191, 196
   promoting high level of
      101, 103
   and the unborn baby 109
   understanding HUFAs and
      their derivatives 94–6
Hippocrates 54
honesty 66
hopelessness 2, 23, 24–5, 32,
   48, 53, 215
hormones 60, 90, 192–3
Horrobin, Professor David F.
   and brain development 80
   high levels of EFAs funda-
      mental to healthy brain
      function 75
   link between intake of
      EFAs and depression vi, 83,
      84
   mood disorders and a diet
      low in EFAs 80–81
   and multiple sclerosis 73
   pregnant women's brains
      109
   research into schizophrenia
      13, 39, 79, 97
   Scottish Study 98
   testing for EFAs 83
   his theory followed up by
      Puri and others 16, 41, 46
HUFA *see* 'highly' unsaturated
   fatty acids

Huntington's chorea, treatment
  with EPA vii, 107–11, 185
hydralazine 74
hydrogenated fats 157, 167
hydrogenation 104, 156
hyperforin 140
Hypericum perforatum see St
  John's wort
hyperthyroidism 33
hypothalamus 90
hypothyroidism 33–4

IBS see irritable bowel
  syndrome
ICD see International
  Classification of Diseases
  and Related Health
  Problems
imipramine (Tofranil; Janimine)
  134
inadequacy 32, 36
indinavir 141
infections 102
insomnia 225
  see also sleep patterns
insulin 203
International Classification of
  Diseases and Related
  Health Problems (ICD)
  (latest edition ICD–10)
  30–31
Internet 15, 116, 149, 150,
  151, 222–3
introversion 67
iofepramine (Gamanil) 134
irritability 28, 36, 40, 48
irritable bowel syndrome (IBS)
  32
isocarboxazid (Marplan) 135
isolation 4, 8, 26, 27, 31, 66–8

Janimine 134
jaundice 132

LA see linoleic acid
lack of energy 25
lethargy 31, 35, 72, 215
Levodopa 74
libido (sex drive) 6, 28, 36, 50,
  102
lifestyle 4, 60, 75, 186, 230
light therapy 35, 39, 117
linoleic acid (LA) 93, 94, 96–7
  sources of 95, 169, 170
  see also omega-6
lipids 93
lithium carbonate 37, 117
liver 92
liver enzymes 141
loneliness 62, 66
loss 56–7, 64–6, 143
loss of interest and pleasure in
  life 25, 30, 31, 48
Ludiomil 135
Lustral 130
Luvox 130

mackerel 9, 163, 164, 165–6
macular degenerative disease
  (MDD) 192
magnesium 73, 103, 173, 174
magnetic resonance imaging
  (MRI) 105, 106–7, 200
major depression see severe
  depression
malaria 4
mania 36–7, 91
manic depression see bipolar
  disorder
MAOIs see monoamine
  oxidase inhibitors
maprotiline (Ludiomil) 135
marlin 165
Marplan 135
Marshall, Dr Barry 12–13
Marx, Karl 46
massage 179, 210, 224–5

mastalgia 193
Maxepa TM 149
ME *see* myalgic
    encephalomyelitis
meditation 178, 227–8
melancholia 54
melatonin 73, 91
Mellor, Jan 39
memory 91
men
    depressed men and heart
        disease 21
    single/married 42
    suicide in young men 21,
        42, 43
mianserin 135
migraine 32, 225
mild depression 14, 53, 121,
    150
    diagnosis 31
    EPA dosage 152–3
    ICD classification 31
mineral deficiency vii
mirtazapine (Zispin; Remeron)
    132
moderate depression 14, 22,
    53, 121, 150
    diagnosis 31
    EPA dosage 152–3
    ICD classification 31
Molipaxin 133
Monash University, Australia
    108
monoamine oxidase inhibitors
    (MAOIs) 5, 124, 125, 129,
    135–6, 137, 141
monoamine theory 120, 122–8
    chance discovery of the first
        antidepressants 123–4
    problems with the theory
        126–8
        the action of reserpine
            127–8

the delay in the time the
    antidepressant takes to
    act 126–7
the theory 125–6
monounsaturated fats 159
mood
    change in 47–8, 50
    low 2, 8, 23, 24, 35, 48, 53,
        67, 99, 100, 180
    mood swings 37, 43, 63, 73,
        161
mood-stabilising drugs 74
Morepa TM 149
Morgan, Elaine 78
MRI *see* magnetic resonance
    imaging
multiple sclerosis 73
myalgic encephalomyelitis
    (ME) 199, 201
myelin sheath 73

nails
    brittle 102
    EPA of benefit to health of
        vii, 145
    weak 173–4
Narcotics Anonymous 211
Nardil 135
NARIs *see* Selective
    Noradrenaline Re-uptake
    Inhibitors
NaSSAs *see* Noradrenergic
    and Specific Serotonergic
    Antidepressants
National Health Service
    (NHS) 31, 119, 120, 149
natural treatments for depres-
    sion, other 139–44
    cognitive analytical therapy
        (CAT) 140, 142–4, 147
        EPA alongside CAT 144
        how effective is it?
            143–4

St John's wort 140–42, 144, 145
how does it compare with EPA? 142, 146–7
how effective is it? 141
what are the side effects? 141–2
'nature versus nurture' 44
Nefazodone (Dutonin; Serzone) 133
negative thinking 28, 49, 50, 55, 58–9, 143
Nemets, Dr Boris 99
neurons 88, 89, 90, 93, 94, 100, 101, 106, 111, 124, 125, 127, 132
neurotransmitters 72, 89–90, 101, 106
and antidepressants 5, 123, 126–7, 128
and HUFAs 94
low levels of 5, 61, 100, 125
monoamine 124, 126
Newton, Sir Isaac: Principia viii
nicotine
hampers EPA production vii
increased intake 28
see also smoking
noradrenaline (norepinephrine) 5, 61, 72, 89–90, 100, 111, 124, 125, 131–5, 140
Noradrenergic and Specific Serotonergic Antidepressants (NaSSAs) 132, 136
nortriptyline (Allegron; Aventyl; Pamelor) 134
nutrition
levels 104
poor nutrition and depression 159–61
obesity 157

obsessive/compulsive behaviour 27
oestrogens 193
oils 92, 156, 159, 166–7
older people at risk 43, 53
olfactory hallucinations 29
omega-3 fatty acids vi, 9, 111, 158, 162, 163, 166, 187
the body's need for vii
deficiency vii, 167
and diet vii
pathway 95, 96
and psoriasis 191
and rheumatoid arthritis 196–7
sources of 167, 168, 171, 172
vital for overall brain health 92
see also alpha-linolenic acid
omega-3 type HUFAs 94
omega-6 fatty acids 111, 158, 162
beneficial effects on skin and hair 191
pathway 95–6
sources of 168, 169, 170
vital for overall brain health 92
see also linoleic acid
omega-6 type HUFAs 94
ongoing depressed mood 30, 31
openness 214
oral contraceptive pill 6, 74, 141
orangutans 76
orgasm 6
osteoarthritis 196

pain
chronic 71
emotional 91

painkillers 74
palpitations 33, 72
Pamelor 134
panic attacks 27, 48
paranoia 38, 59, 143
parents, loss of 64–5, 99
Parkinson's disease 43, 72–3, 74
Parnate 135
paroxetine (Seroxat, Paxil) 130
passivity 57, 62
Paxil 130
Peet, Professor Malcolm vi, 39, 83, 98
pentazocine 74
perception 50
peripheral neuropathy 204
personal hygiene 30
pharmaceutical companies see drug companies
pharmacist 116
phenelzine (Nardil) 135
1-phenylalanine 61
phobias 27, 36
phospholipase 97
phospholipid bilayer 93, 97, 156
phospholipid layer 99, 100, 101, 122, 128, 155
phospholipids 93–4, 96, 97, 105, 181, 184
phosphorus 92, 93
physical factors 71–5, 85
    chronic pain 71
    diet 73
    malfunction of the endocrine system 72
    multiple sclerosis 73
    Parkinson's disease 72–3
    prescription drugs 74–5
    Seasonal Affective Disorder (SAD) 73
    stroke 72

pilchards 9
pineal gland 73, 91
pituitary gland 72, 90
placebos 6, 10, 98, 99, 109, 141
plaice 163
PMS see premenstrual syndrome
PND see postnatal depression
pollution 4, 104, 177
polychlorinated biphenyls (PCBs) 165
polyunsaturated fatty acids (PUFA) 93, 159
positive reinforcement, lack of 57–8
postnatal depression (PND) 14, 23, 53
    'baby blues' 35–6
    and EFA supplements 195–6
    and fish consumption 81–2, 81
    postnatal depression 36
    puerperal psychosis 36
    treatment 36
potassium 73
poverty 46, 62
pregnancy 195–6
premenstrual syndrome (PMS) 36, 102, 192–3, 195
priapism 133
problems accessing help 40
processed foods 175, 184
    trans-fatty acids vii, 104, 158
prostaglandins 102, 172, 193
proteins 61, 92
Prozac (fluoxetine) 5–6, 84–5, 118, 119, 125, 130, 136, 140
psoriasis 174, 191
psychiatrists 120
psychoanalysis 142

psychological factors 15, 41, 55, 56–9, 63, 85, 151
helplessness 57
lack of positive reinforcement 57–8
loss 56–7
negative thought patterns 58–9
trying too hard to be good and perfect 59
psychotic symptoms 29, 31, 32, 194
puerperal psychosis 36
PUFA see 'poly' unsaturated fatty acids
pumpkin seeds (Cucurbita pepo) 171
Puri, Dr Basant
breakthrough with EPA 1, 6, 16, 17, 110, 128, 144, 229
first case study using EPA for depression (Anthony) 7–12, 88, 91–2, 98, 104–6, 108
and raising EPA levels 76
successful use of EPA in his clinical practice 12, 98, 120–21
testing for EFAs 82

rapeseed oil (Brassica napus) 169
reactive depression 41, 62
reboxetine (Edronax) 132
recovery from depression 207–20
depression is a journey 230–31
keep informed about your health 222–3
natural therapies to aid your recovery 223
acupuncture 223–4
aromatherapy 225
massage 224–5
protecting your future 220–22
spiritual disciplines to aid your recovery
meditation 227–8
t'ai chi 226–7
yoga 226
stage 1: waiting for EPA to work for you 209–11
stage 2: when EPA starts to take effect 212–16
stage 3: full recovery from depression 217–20
what EPA means for all depression sufferers 229–30
red blood cells (erythrocytes) 82–4, 187
religious belief, lack of 4, 67
Remeron 132
repressed feelings 65–6
research 4–6, 84–5
Israeli Study 99
Scottish Study 98, 99
reserpine 127–8
resistant depression 8
restlessness 38
rheumatoid arthritis 74, 196–8
Richardson, Alex 39
Ritalin 202
routine 212–13

SAD see seasonal affective disorder
St John's wort 6, 15, 113, 140–42, 144, 145, 146–7
salmon 9, 163, 164, 165–6
Samaritans 210
sardines 9, 163, 164, 165
saturated carbon chains 93–4
saturated fat 92, 155–8, 175

and depression 73
and EFAs 38, 97, 103
phospholipids 93
replaced by unsaturated
   EFAs 100
sources of 99–100
Saul 54
schizophrenia 38, 53, 124, 155
   effect of EPA vi vii, 6,
   9–10, 97, 107–8, 110, 111,
   193–5, 199
   and low EFAs 80
   Professor Horrobin's
   research 13, 39, 79, 97
   treatment 39
seasonal affective disorder
   (SAD) 14, 23, 25, 34–5, 39,
   53, 73, 91
   treatment 35, 117, 141
Selective Noradrenaline and
   Serotonin Re-uptake
   Inhibitors (SNRIs) 131,
   136
Selective Noradrenaline Re-
   uptake Inhibitors (NARIs)
   132, 136
Selective Serotonin Re-uptake
   Inhibitors (SSRIs) 5, 85,
   118, 119, 123, 125, 129,
   130–31, 136, 141
   SSRI Withdrawal Syndrome
   137
self–destructive behaviour 28
self–esteem 27, 32, 58, 63, 101,
   144, 151
self–neglect 30
serotonin 5, 61, 72, 84,
   89–90, 100, 106, 111, 124,
   125, 130, 133, 134, 135,
   140
Seroxat 130
sertraline (Lustral, Zoloft) 130
Serzone 133

sesame seeds and oil (Sesamum
   indicum) 170
severe depression 14, 22, 53, 121
   diagnosis 30, 32
   ICD classification 31
   recurrence 21
   and St John's wort 142
sex drive see libido
shame 24, 32, 48, 51
shark 165
shiatsu 224–5
Sinequan 134
skin
   and Addison's disease 34
   and anaemia 33
   corticosteroids 74
   dry, itchy 102
   EPA of benefit to health of
   vii, 145, 191–2, 204
   and hypothyroidism 33
   and trazodone 133
sleep patterns 8, 25–6, 35, 36,
   38, 48, 50, 91, 178–9, 199
sleeping pills 29, 74, 127
smoking vii, 63, 73, 83, 100,
   103, 176, 186, 187
   and EFAs 181–3, 184
   increased 49
   see also nicotine
SNRIs see Selective
   Noradrenaline and
   Serotonin Re-uptake
   Inhibitors 131
social class 83
social deprivation 45–6, 53
social factors 4, 41, 62–71, 63,
   85
   addiction and depression
   69–71
   coping with change 68–9
   isolation 66–8
   loss 64–6
   repressed feelings 65–6

social network
  isolation from 31, 48
  rejoining 213
soya beans (Glycine max) 171
speech patterns, changes in 30
SSRIs *see* Selective Serotonin
  Re-uptake Inhibitors
Stahl, Dr Ziva 99
stem cells 12, 106
stigma of mental illness 3, 53,
  230
stomach ulcers 12–13, 33
stress 48, 55, 62, 176
  avoiding 211
  and social deprivation 45
  stress hormones vii, 91, 215,
  224
stroke 43, 72, 189–90, 204
Sudden Infant Death
  Syndrome 196
sugar 73, 103
suicidal thoughts 8, 9, 11, 29,
  50, 210
suicide
  and fish intake 82
  risk of 32, 40, 52
  and SSRIs 119, 131
  statistics 21
  and substance abuse 70
  young men 21, 42, 43
sulphonamide antibiotics 74
sunflower seeds and oil
  (Helianthus anuus) 169
supplementing with EPA
  vii–viii, 15, 17, 43, 86, 101,
  116, 138, 144–7, 148, 149–64
  almonds and almond oil
  (Prunus amygdalus) 171
  cooking suggestions 164–8
    balancing omega-3 and
    omega-6 in our diet
    166–7
    breakfast 168

other foods containing
EPA and EFAs 167–8
safety issues relating to
fish intake 165–6
extra virgin olive oil (Olea
europea) 170
flax oil (linseed) (Linum
usitatissumum) 168–9
foods to avoid, which help
block the metabolism of
EFAs 175–6
how best to buy, store and
cook food to maximise
EFA levels 173
how to treat your depres-
sion with a high EPA
supplement 150–54
EPA dosage 152–4
  for mild to moderate
  depression 152–3780
  to avoid further depressive episodes 153–4
lifestyle factors that affect
levels of EFAs in your body
176–84
ageing and EFAs 183–4
alcohol and EFAs 179–81
high adrenaline (epineph-
rine) caused by stress
176–9
smoking and EFAs 181–3
medicinal sources of EFAs
blackcurrant seed oil (Ribes
nigrum) 172
borage oil (Borago officinalis) Starflower 172
evening primrose oil
(Oenothera biennis) 172
pumpkin seeds (Cucurbita
pepo) 171
raising your EFA levels
with diet and lifestyle
155–64

direct and indirect dietary sources of EPA 162–3
foods we should eat to maximise our EPA and EFA levels 161–2
healthy fats 159
not all fats are bad 157–8
oily fish as a dietary source of EPA 163–4
poor nutrition and depression 159–61
the problem with the modern diet 155–6
a typical daily menu for a modern adult in Britain 156–7
unhealthy fats 158
rapeseed oil (Brassica napus) 169
sesame seeds and oil (Sesamum indicum) 170
soya beans (Glycine max) 171
sunflower seeds and oil (Helianthus anuus) 169
vitamins and minerals that enhance absorption of fatty acids 173–4
walnut oil (Juglans regia) 169
Surmontil 134
swordfish 165
symptoms of depression
anxiety and panic attacks 27
appetite changes 27
difficulty concentrating and making decisions 26
disturbed sleep patterns 25–6
feeling worthless 26–7
feelings of despair and hopelessness 24–5
impatience and irritability 28
lack of energy 25
loss of interest and pleasure in life 25
loss of libido 28
persistent low mood 24
persistent negative thoughts 28
psychotic symptoms 29
self-destructive behaviour 28
suicidal thoughts 29
synapses 89, 127

t'ai chi 221, 226–7
tea vii, 178
tearfulness 25, 36
technology 4
teenagers
and ADHD 203
depression 51, 52
tetracyclic antidepressants 135
thirst 102
thyroid disorder 7, 32, 33–4, 72
thyroid gland 72, 90
thyroxine 34, 72
tiredness 25, 26, 31, 33, 34, 48, 50
Tofranil 134
traditional Chinese medicine (TCM) 223
tranquillisers 127–8
trans-fatty acids vii, 103, 104, 156, 157, 158
tranylcypromine (Parnate) 135
trazodone (Molipaxin; Desyrel; Trialodine) 133
Trialodine 133
tricyclics 5, 124, 125, 129, 134, 137
trimipramine (Surmontil) 134
Triptafen 134
trout 163, 165, 166

1-tryptophan 61
tuberculosis (TB) 124
tuna 9, 163, 164
twin research 44–5
tyramine 136

unemployment 45
unhappiness 66, 143, 179
United States
    lack of diagnosis/treatment
    of depression 19
    level of depression in 3, 43
University of Wales College of
    Medicine, Cardiff 44–5
unresponsiveness 40
unsaturated fat 92, 93, 159
urinary frequency 102

Vaddadi, Krishna 39, 108
Van Gogh, Vincent 46
VegEPA TM 149
vegetable oils 166–7
vegetarians 149, 153, 167
venlafaxine (Efexor; Effexor)
    131, 138
Vipissana meditation 227
vitamins
    deficiency hampers EPA
    production vii
    and EFA levels 103–4

vitamin B6 103, 173
vitamin B complex 73, 174
vitamin C 73
vitamin E 170

walnut oil (Juglans regia) 169,
    184
warfarin 141, 189
weight gain 27, 33
weight loss 7, 8, 27, 30, 34
wheat 73
WHO see World Health
    Organisation
withdrawal 57, 62
women
    a pregnant woman's brain
    109
    rate of depression 15, 41–2,
    53
World Health Organisation
    (WHO) 3–4, 30, 155
worthlessness 26–7

yoga 221, 226

zinc 103, 173–4
Zispin 132
Zoloft 130
Zonalon 134